This book belongs to:

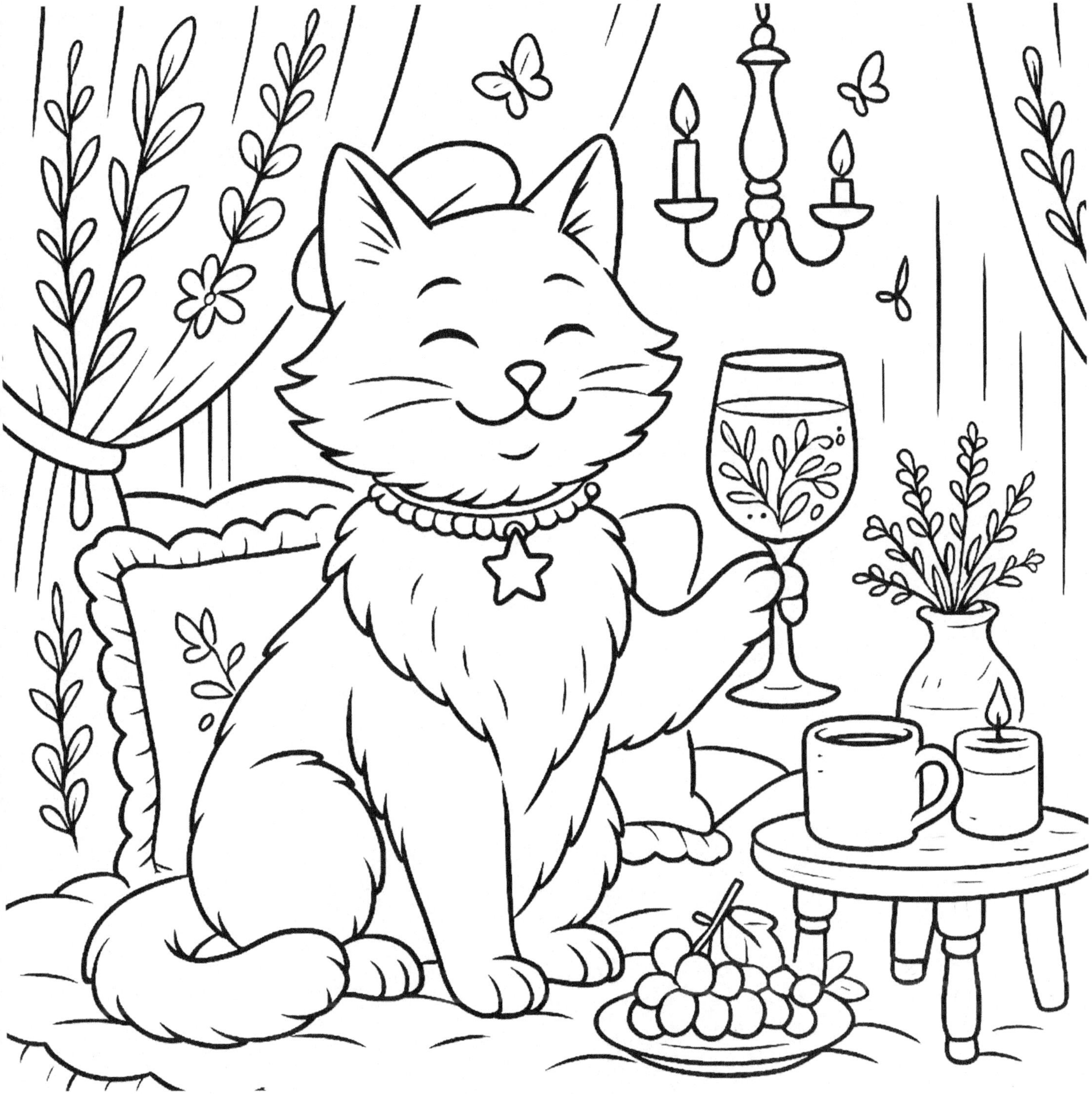

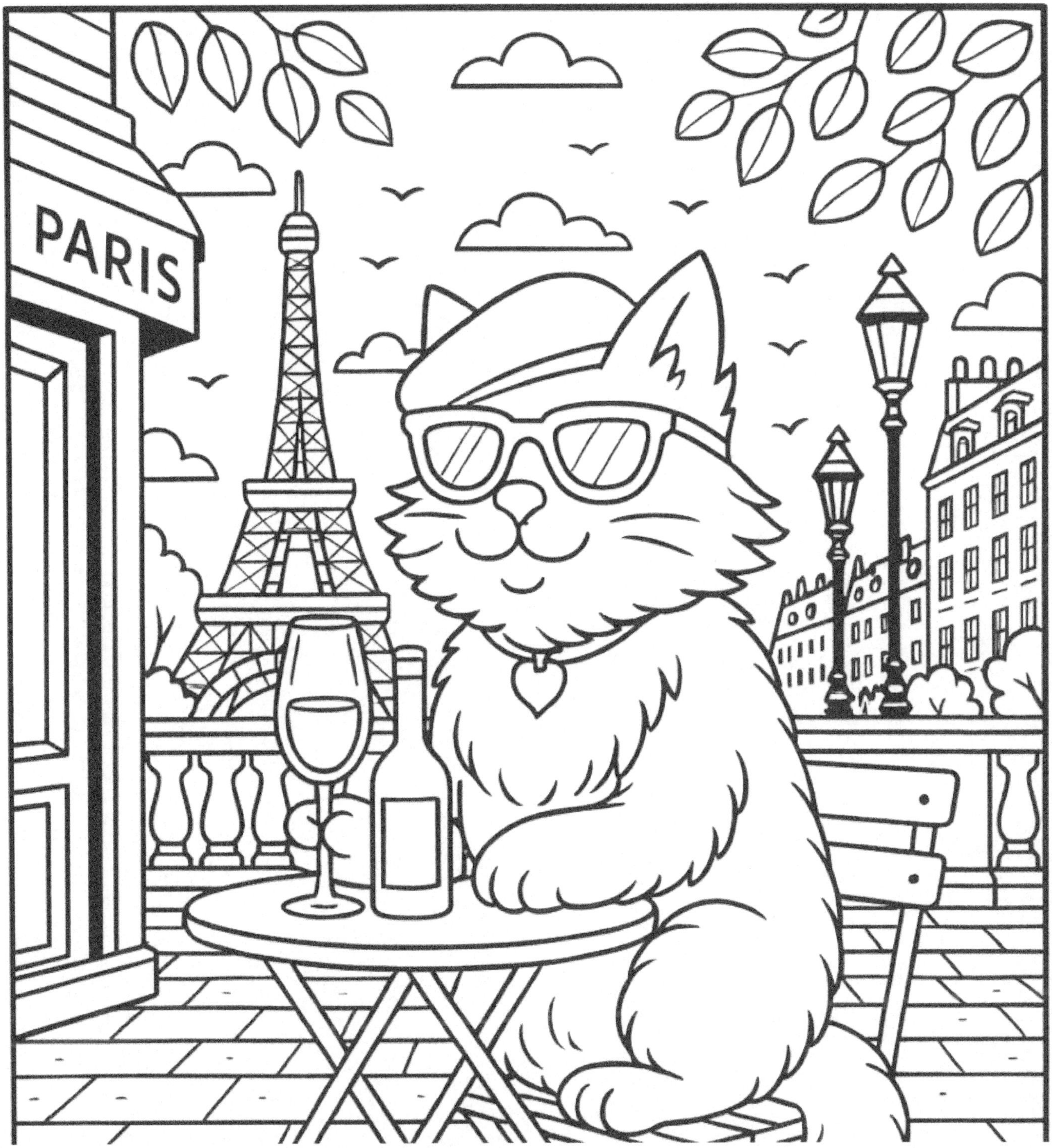
PARIS

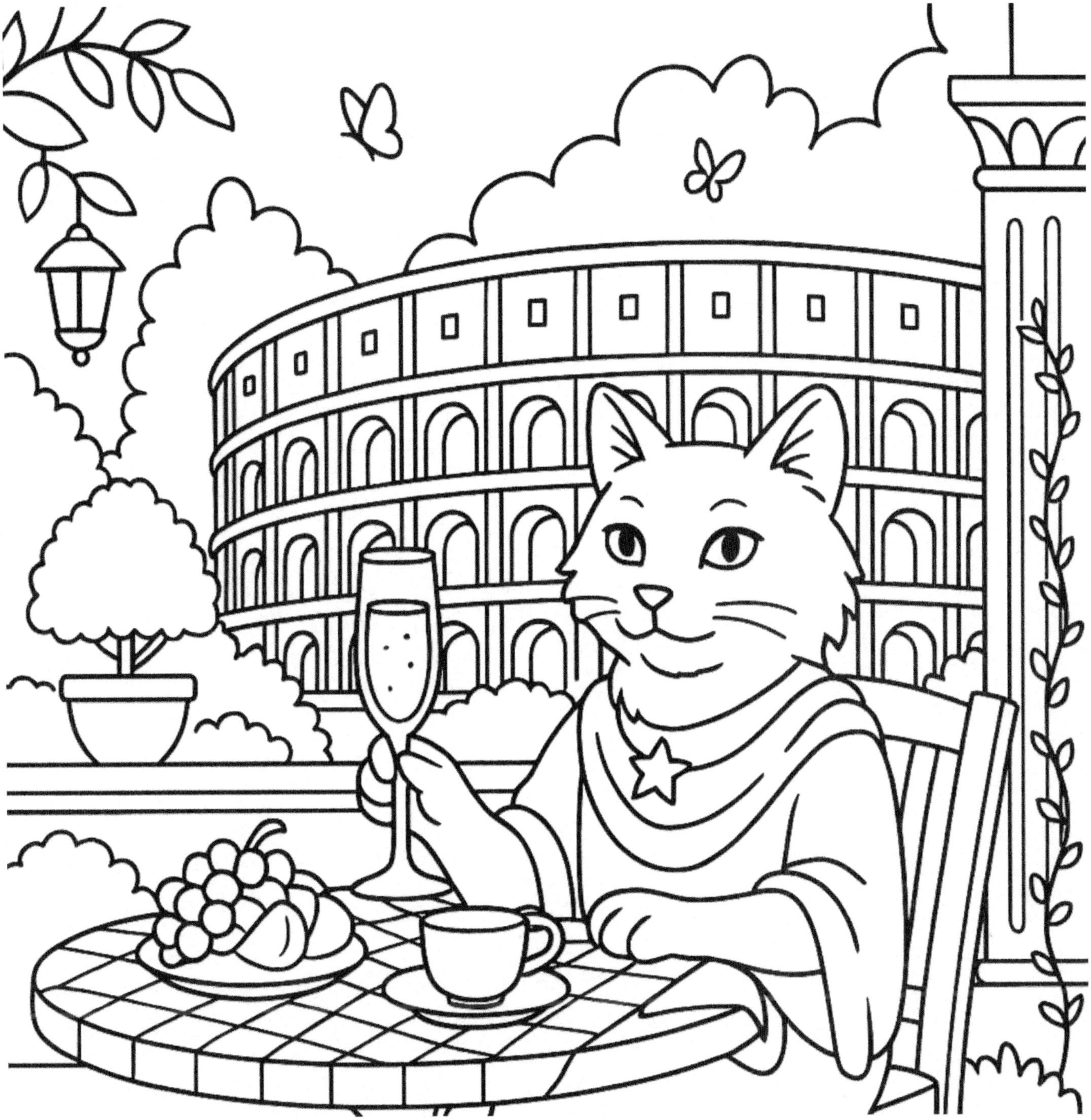

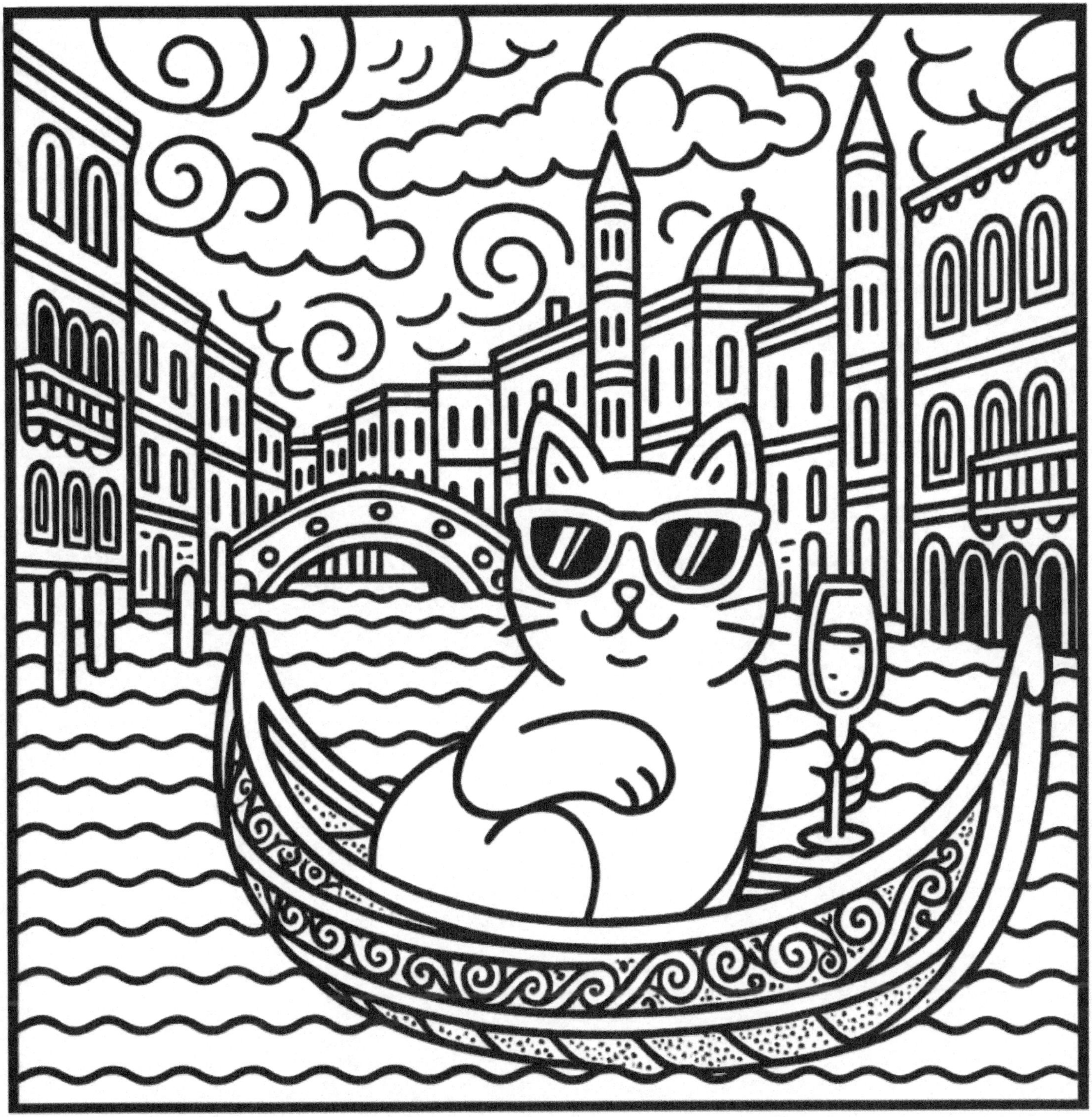

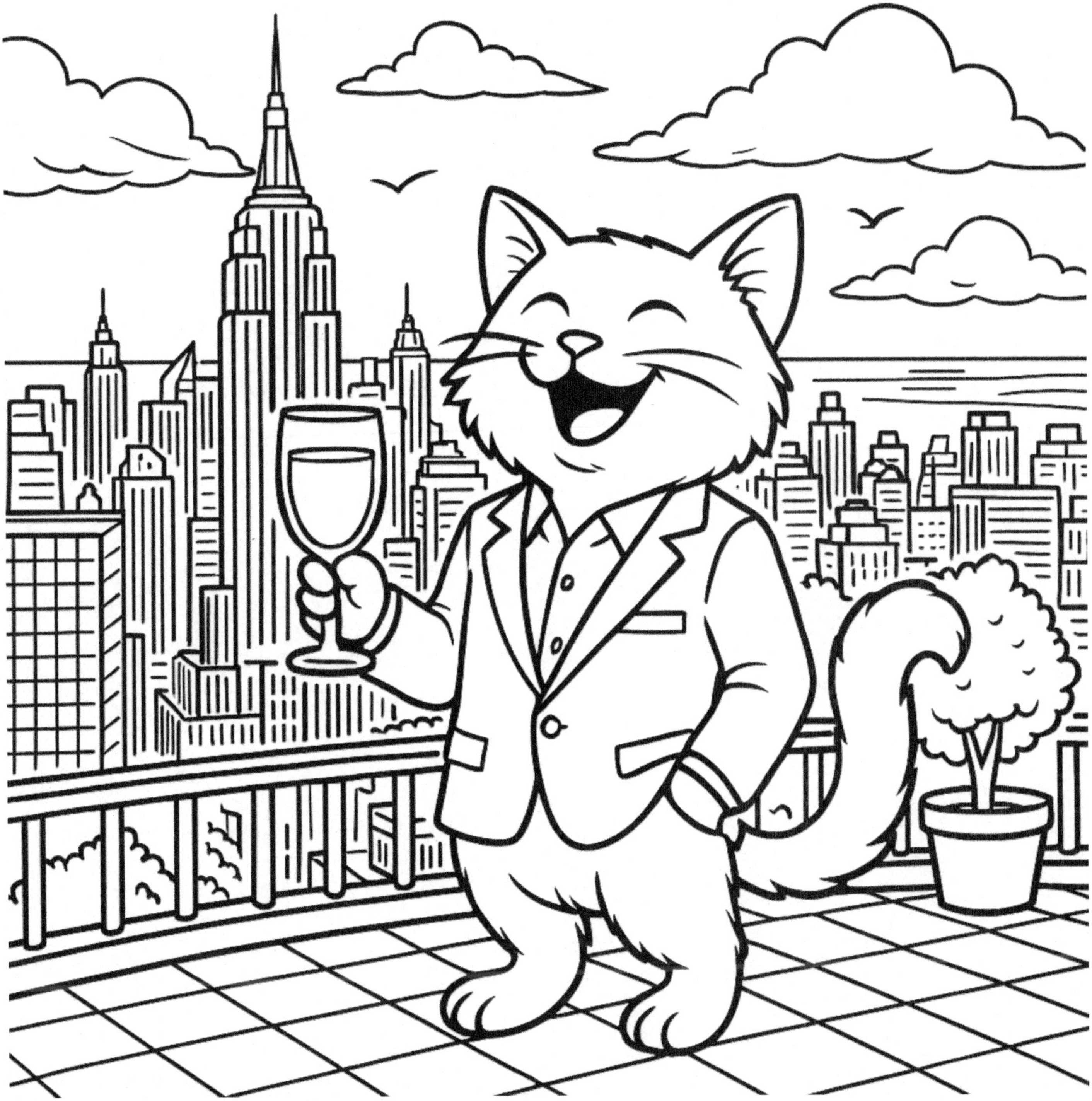

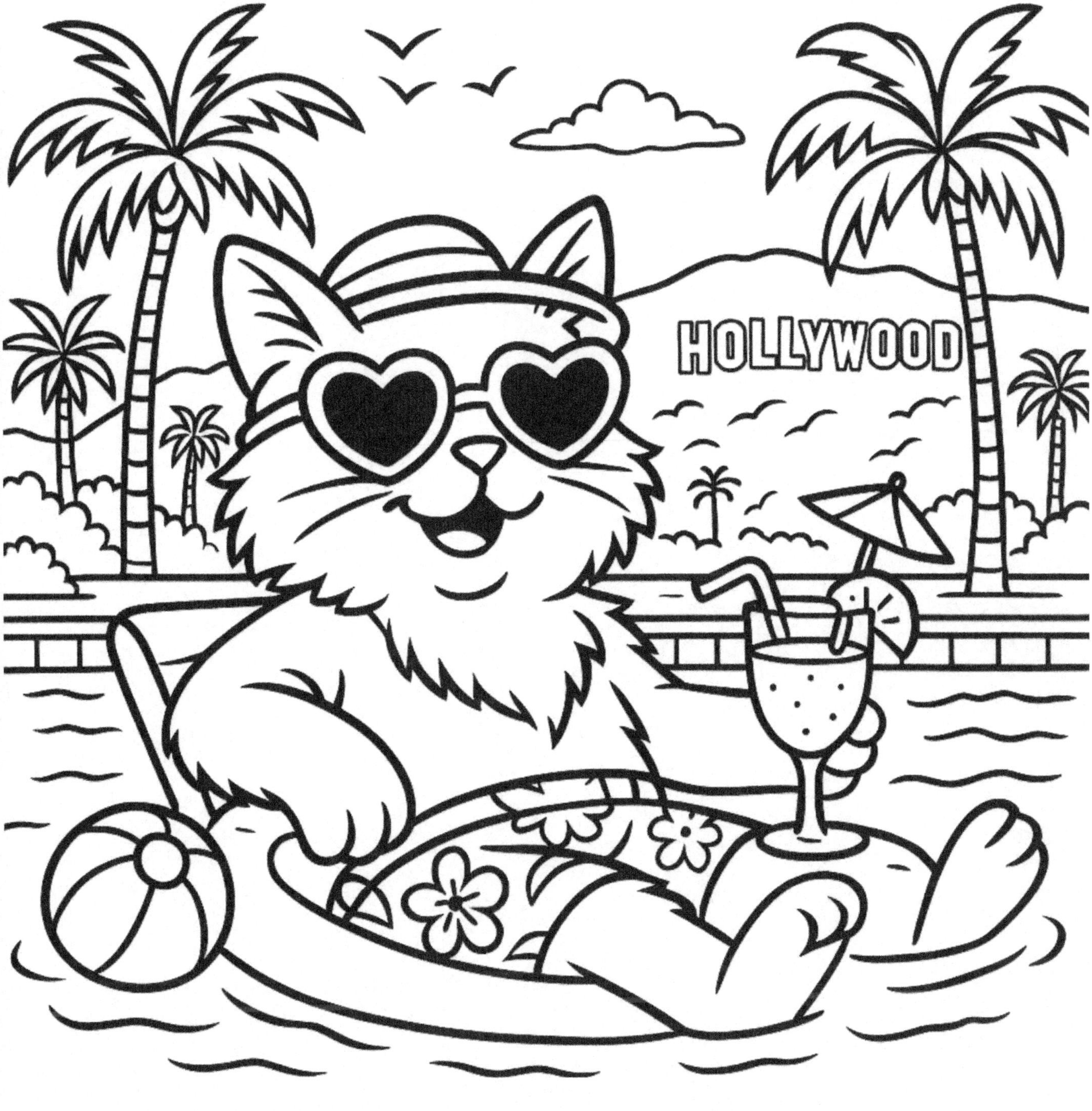
HOLLYWOOD

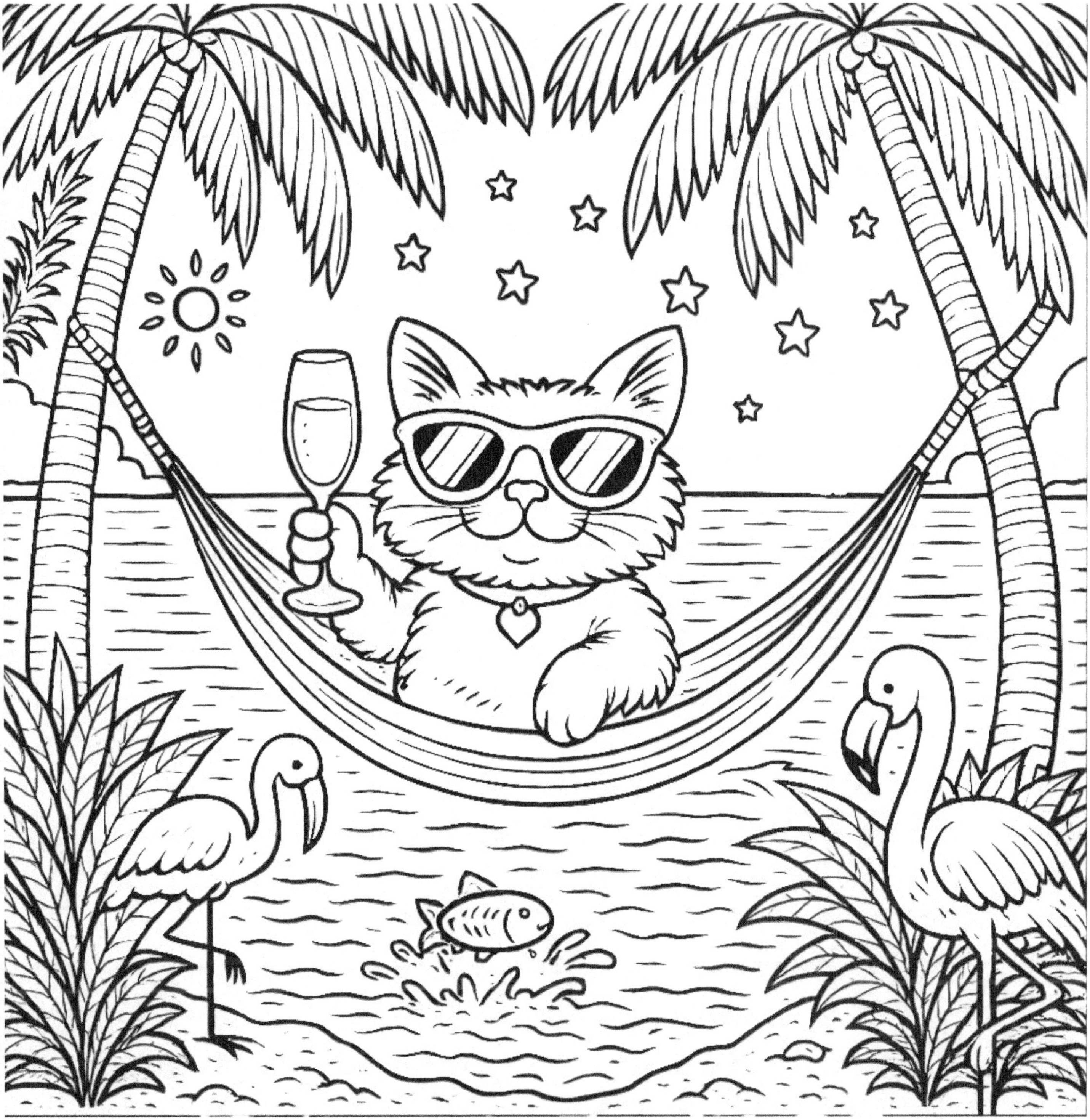

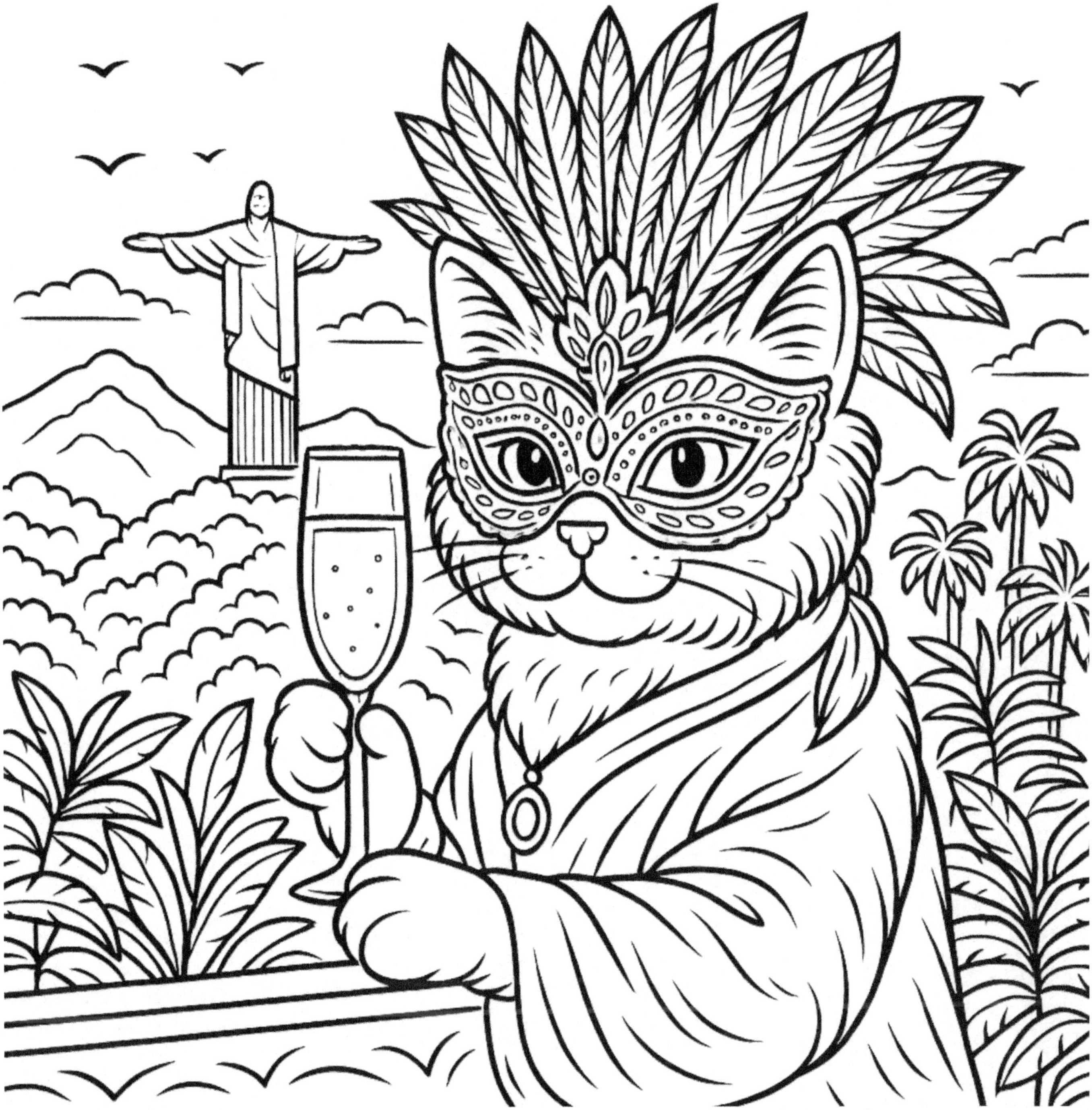

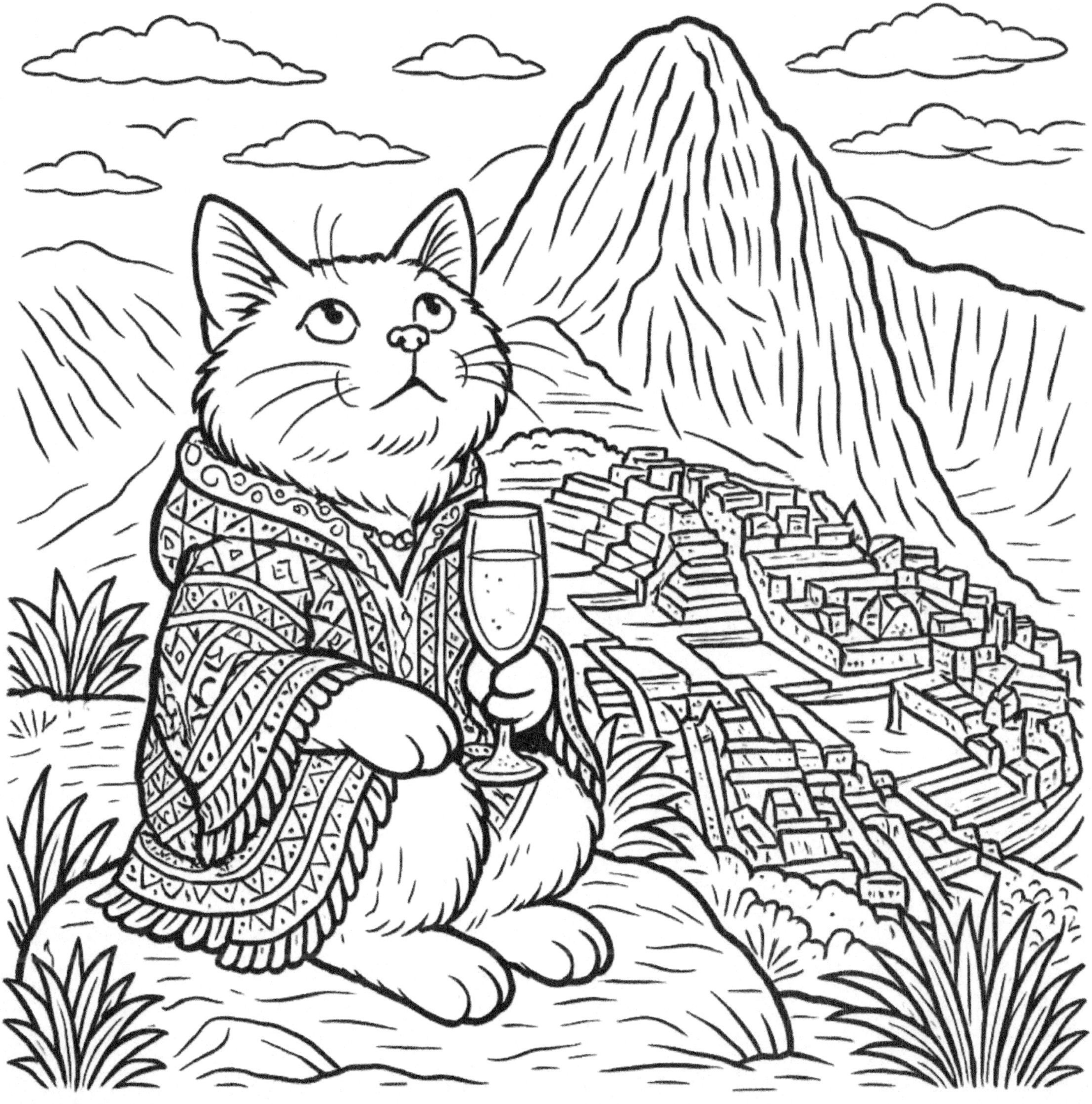

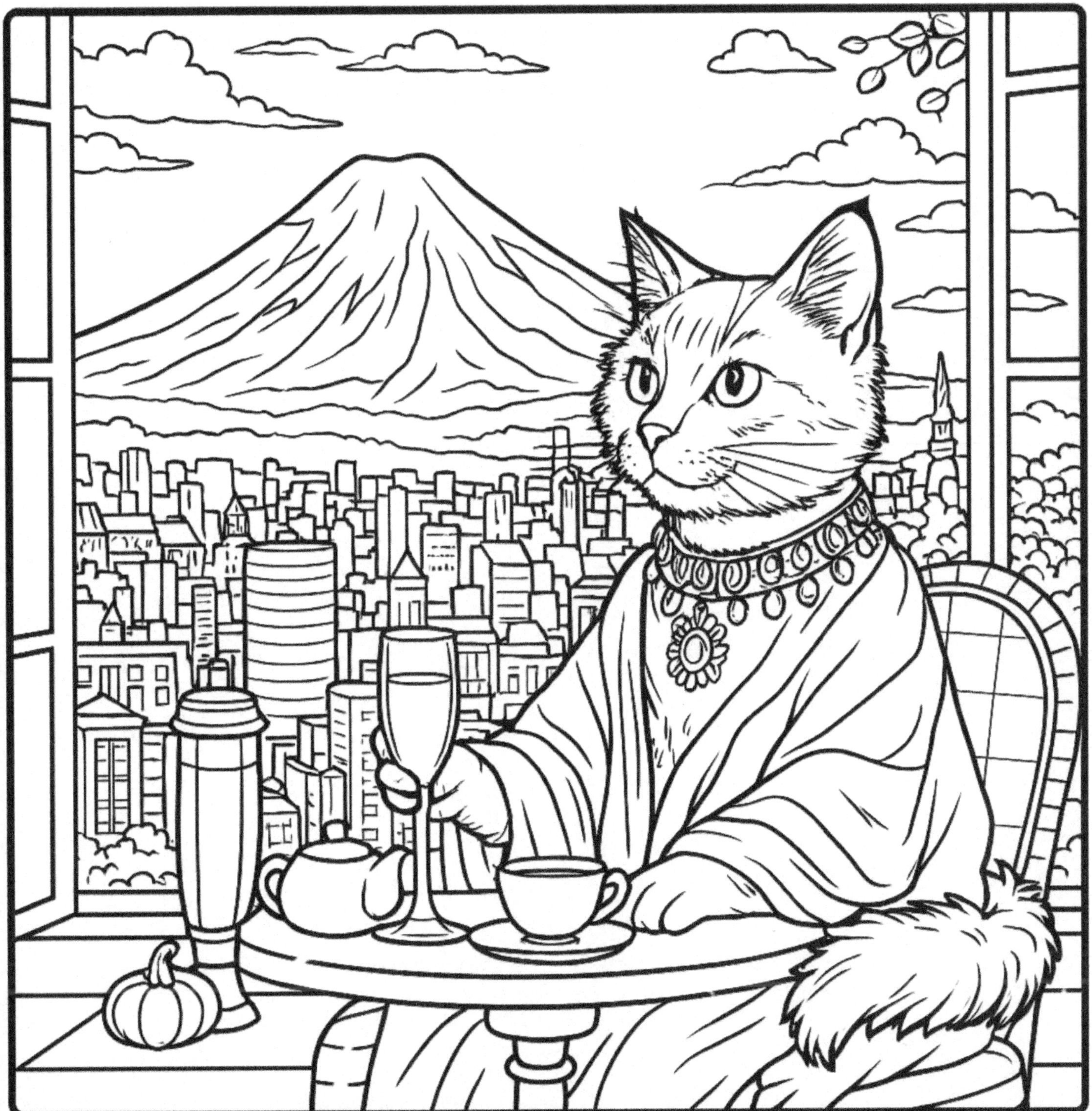

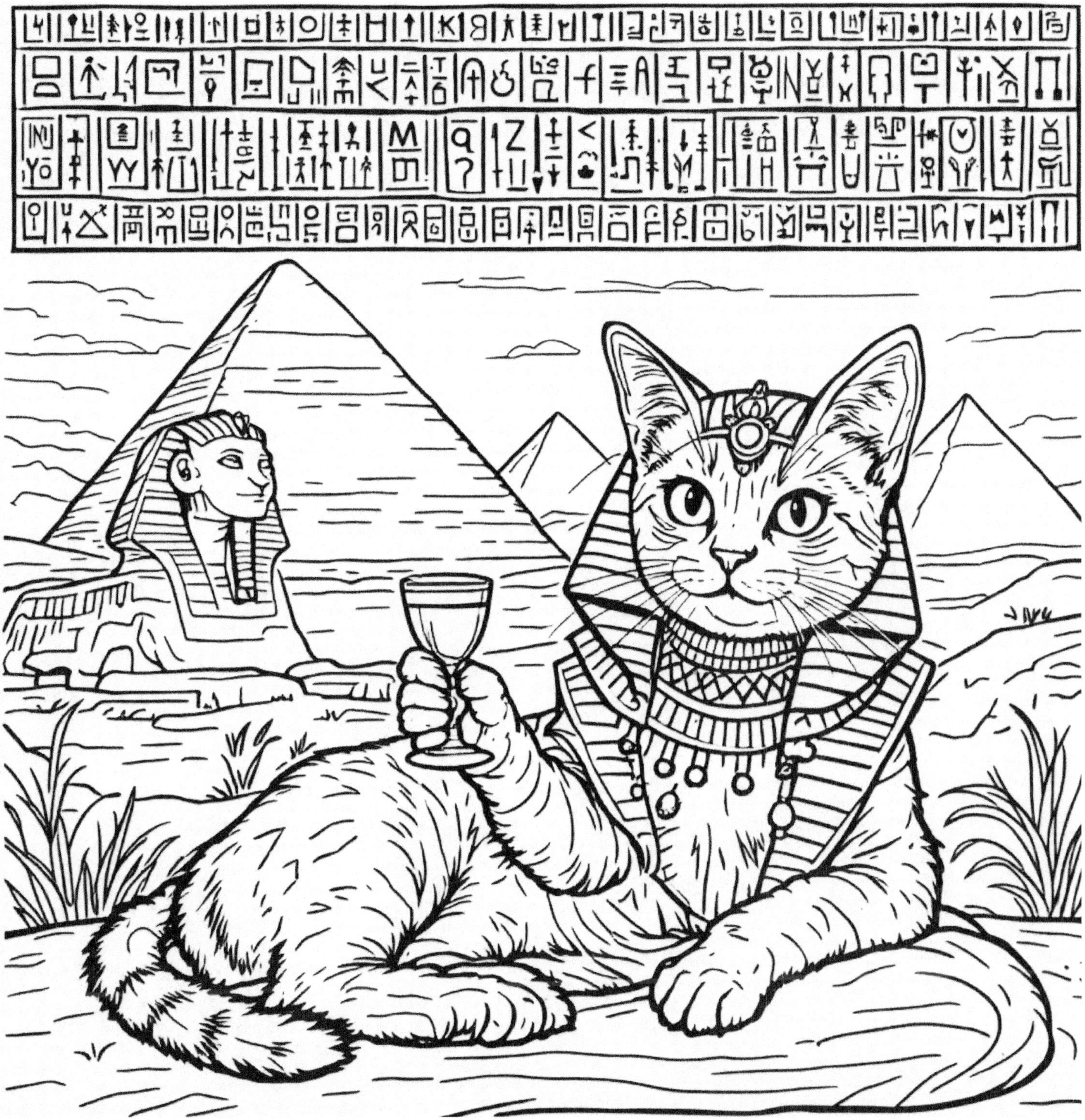

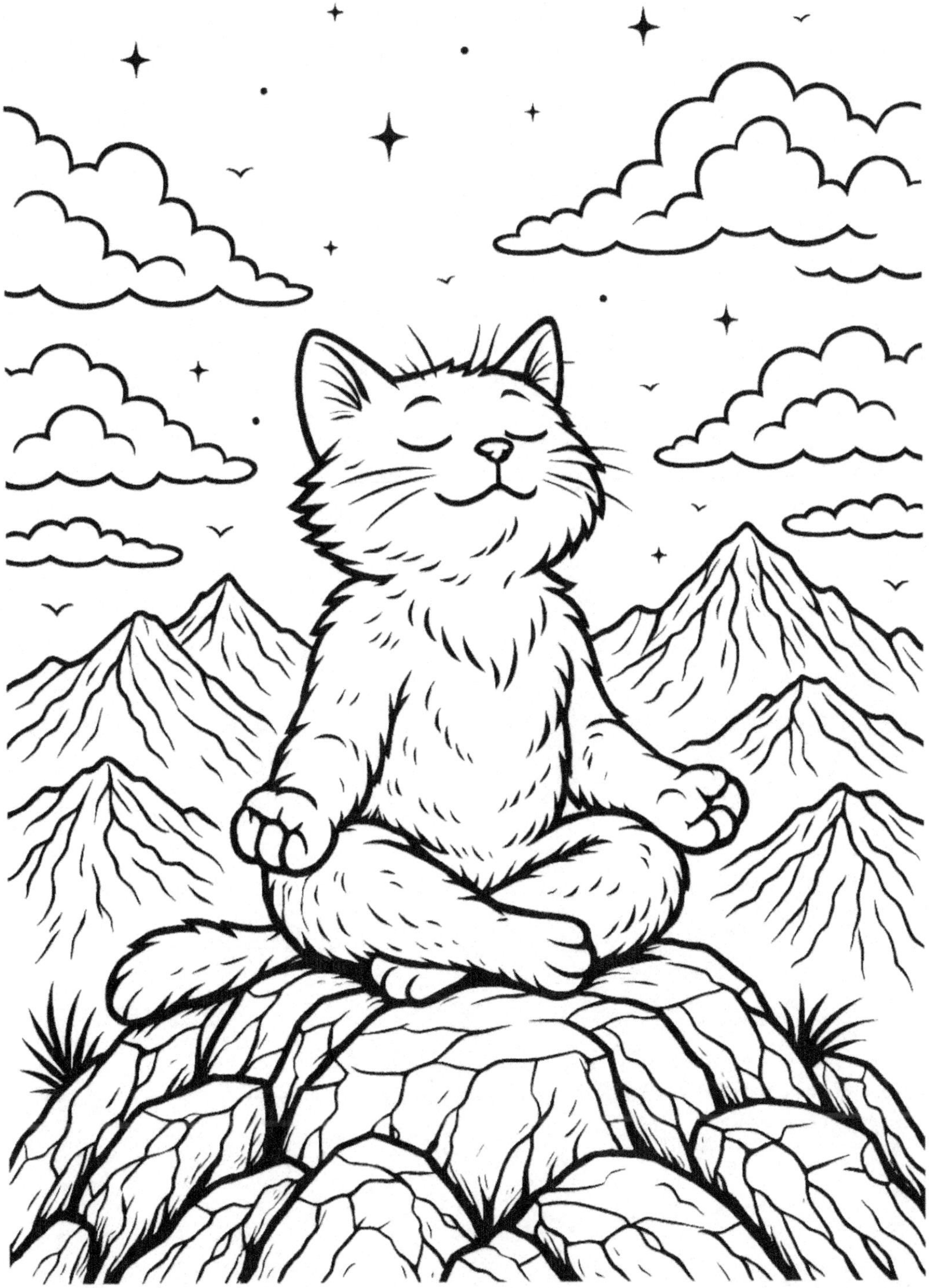

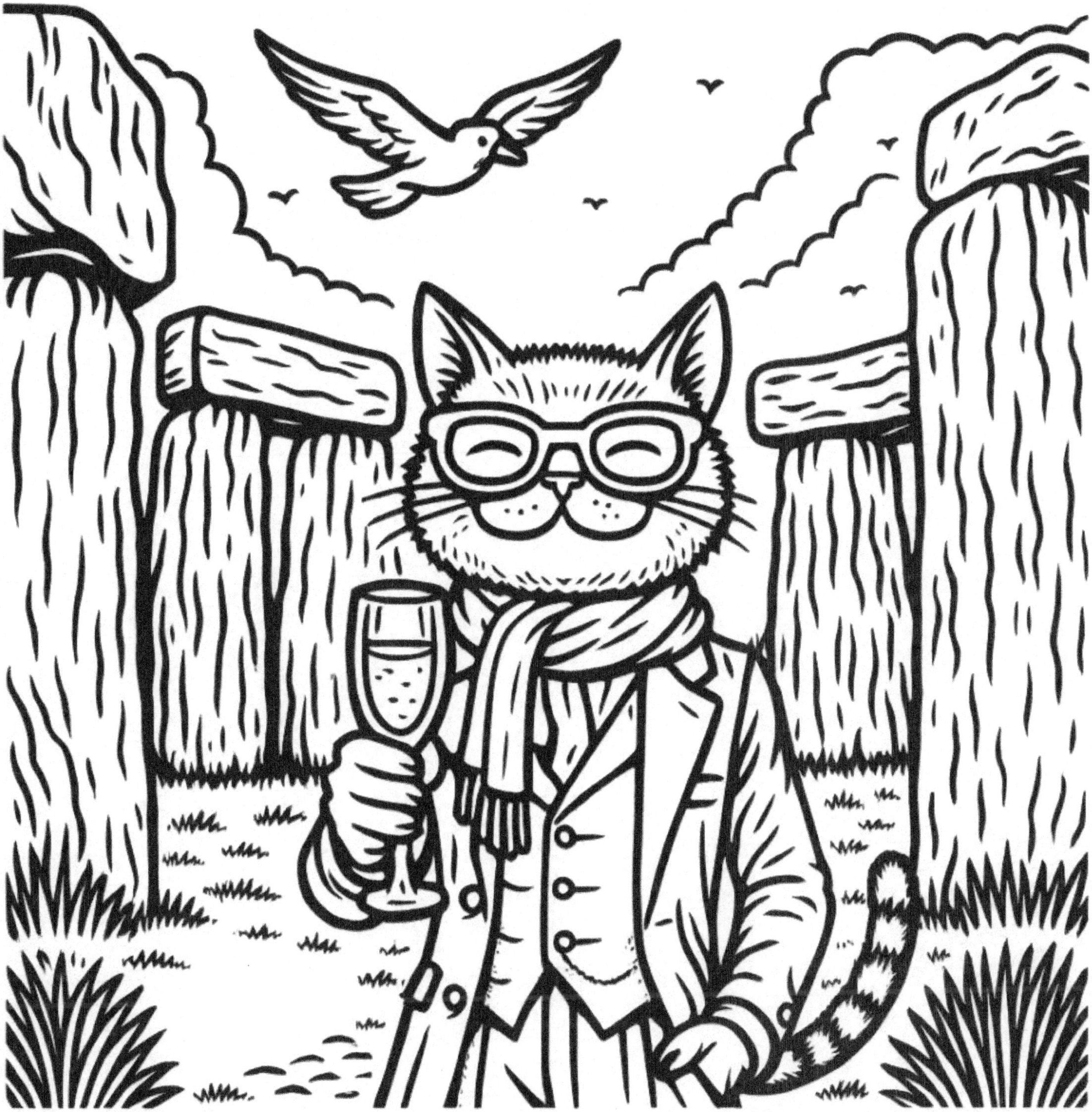

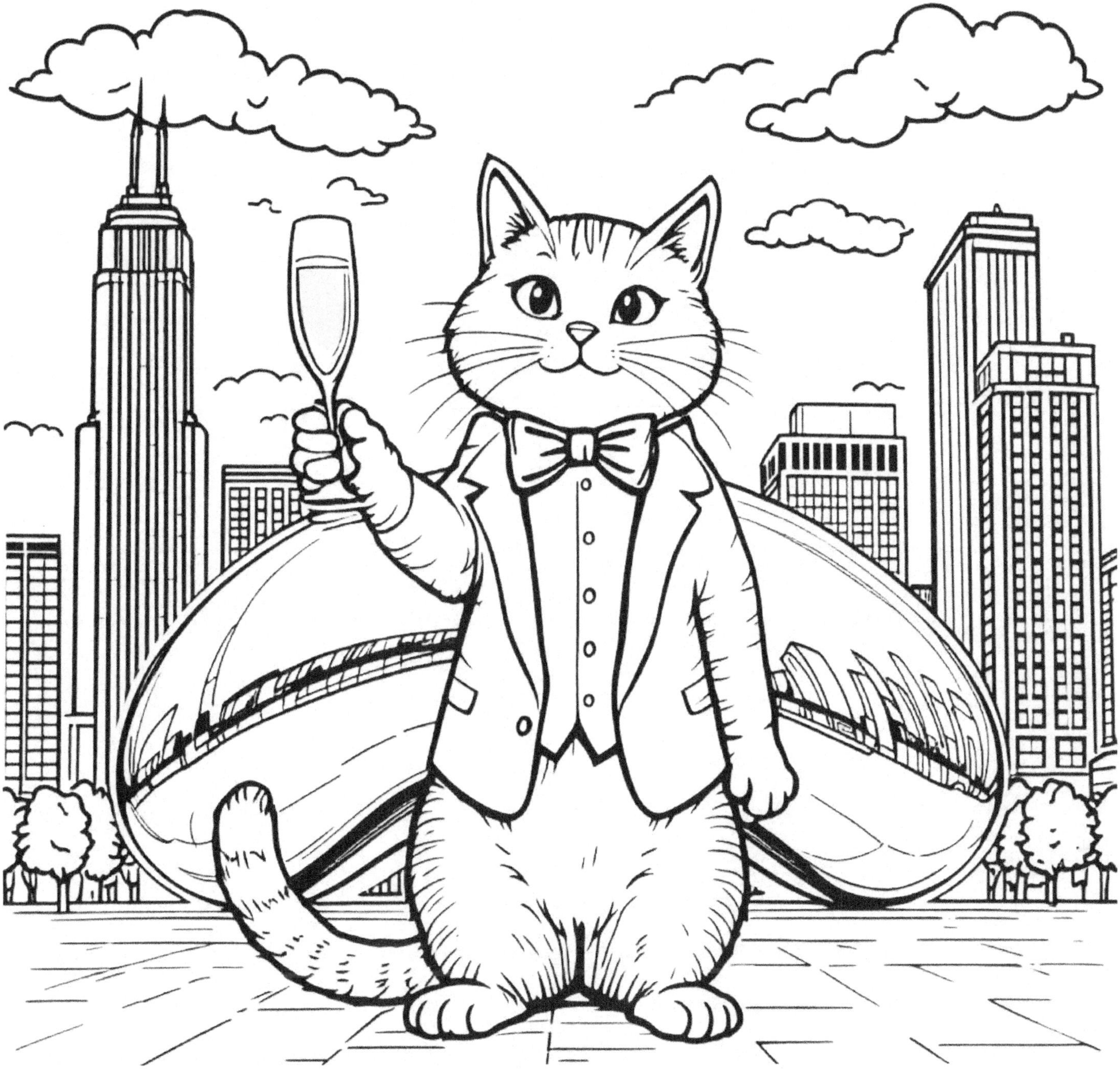

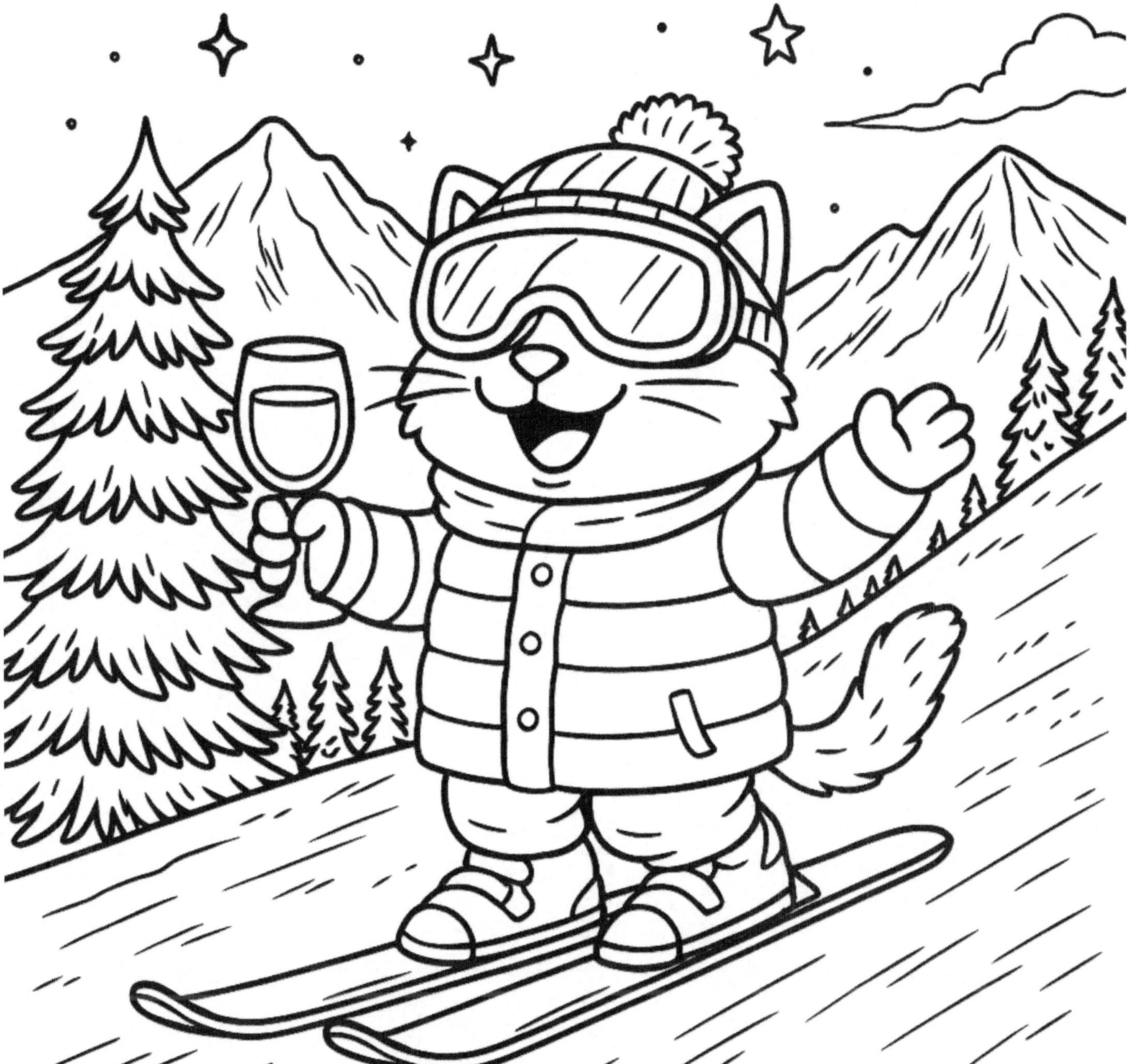

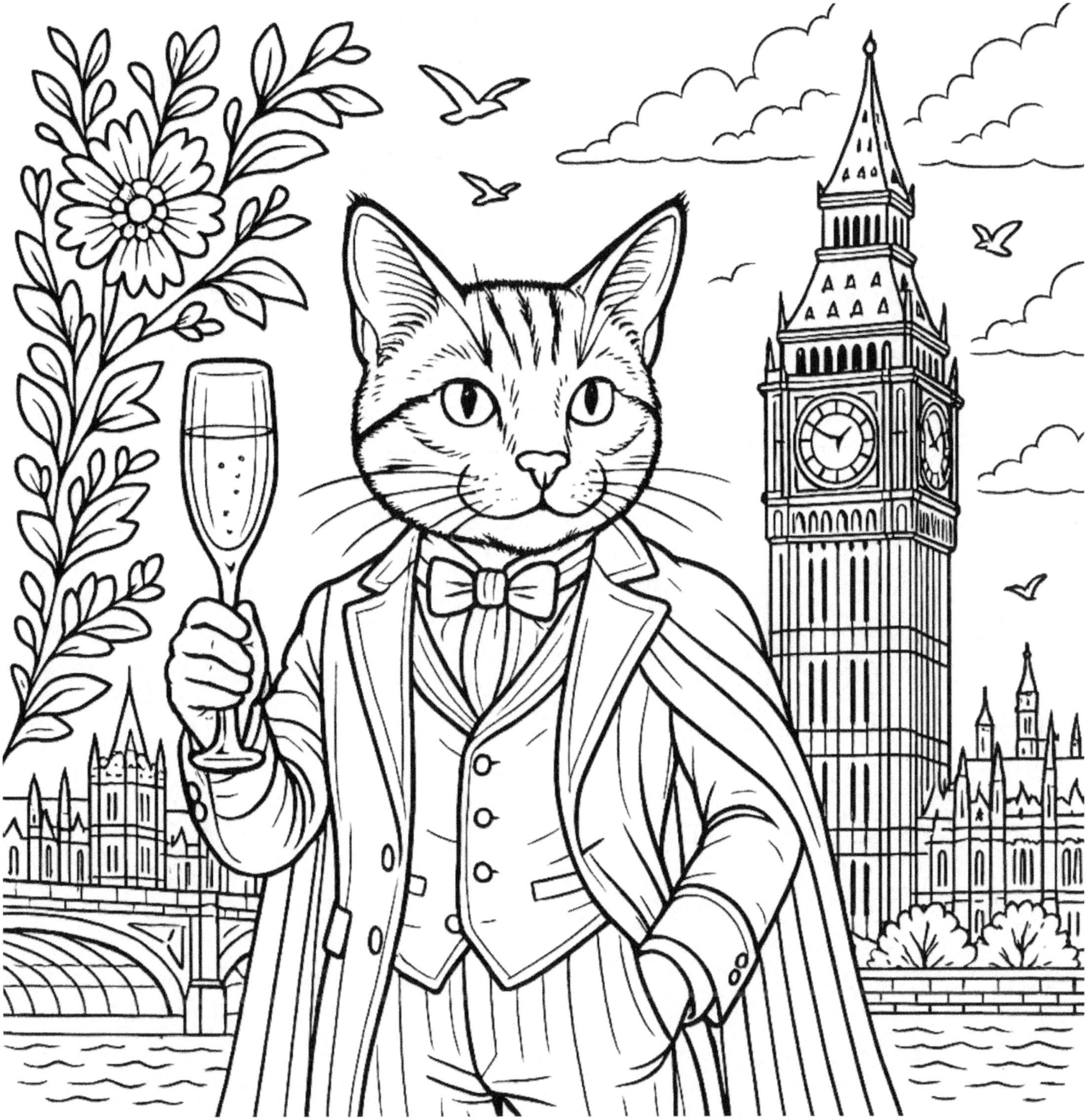

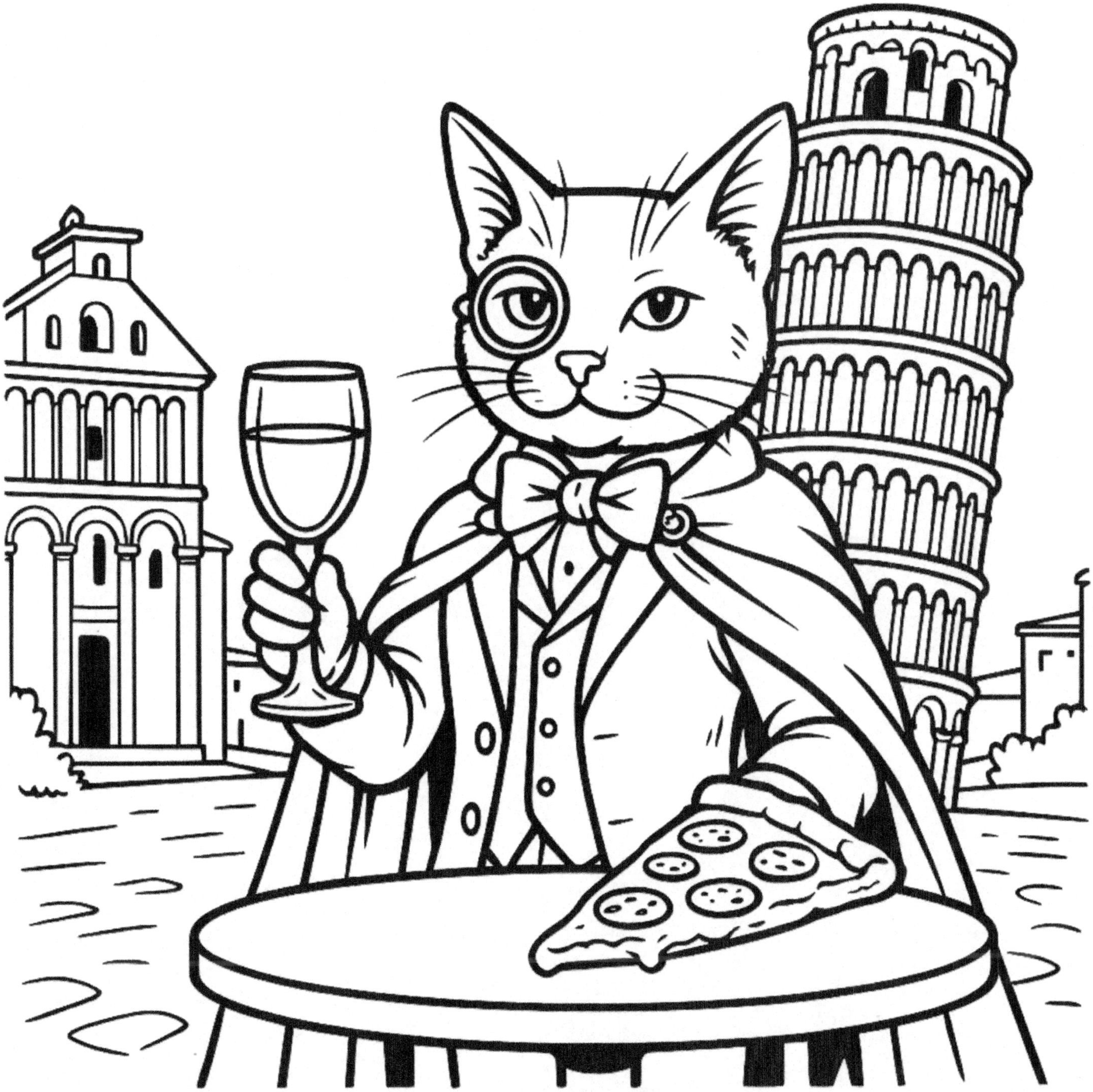

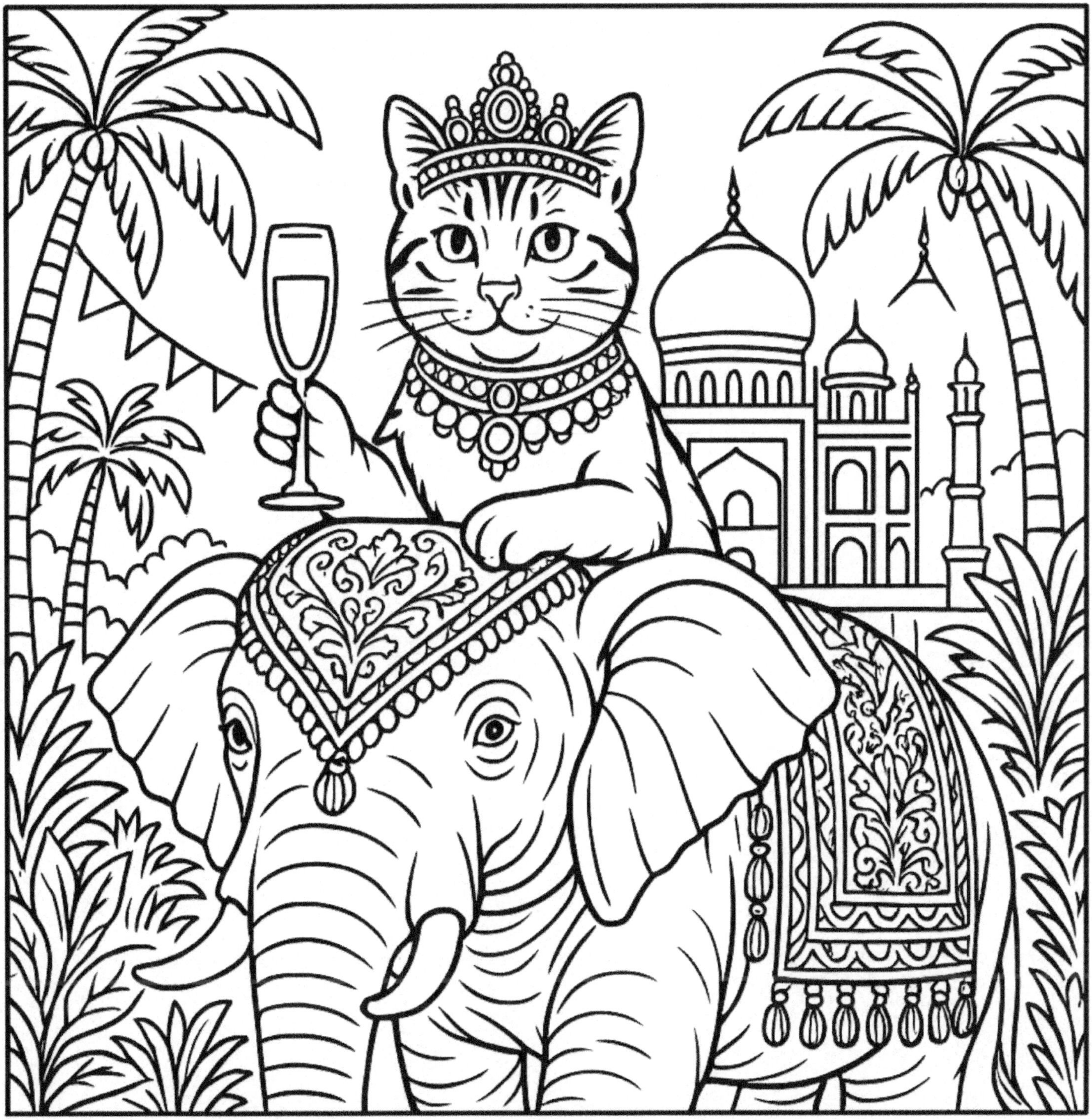

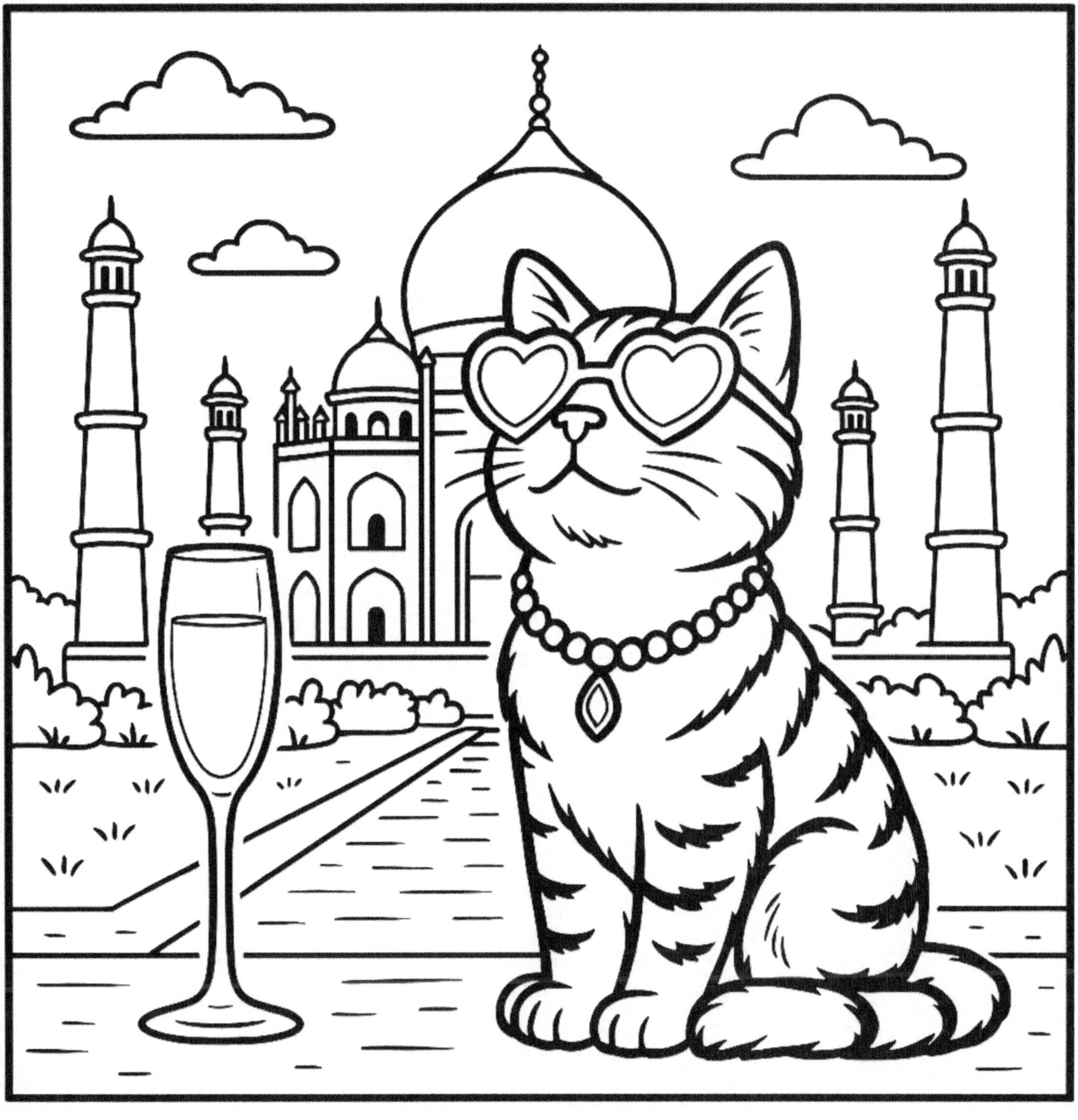

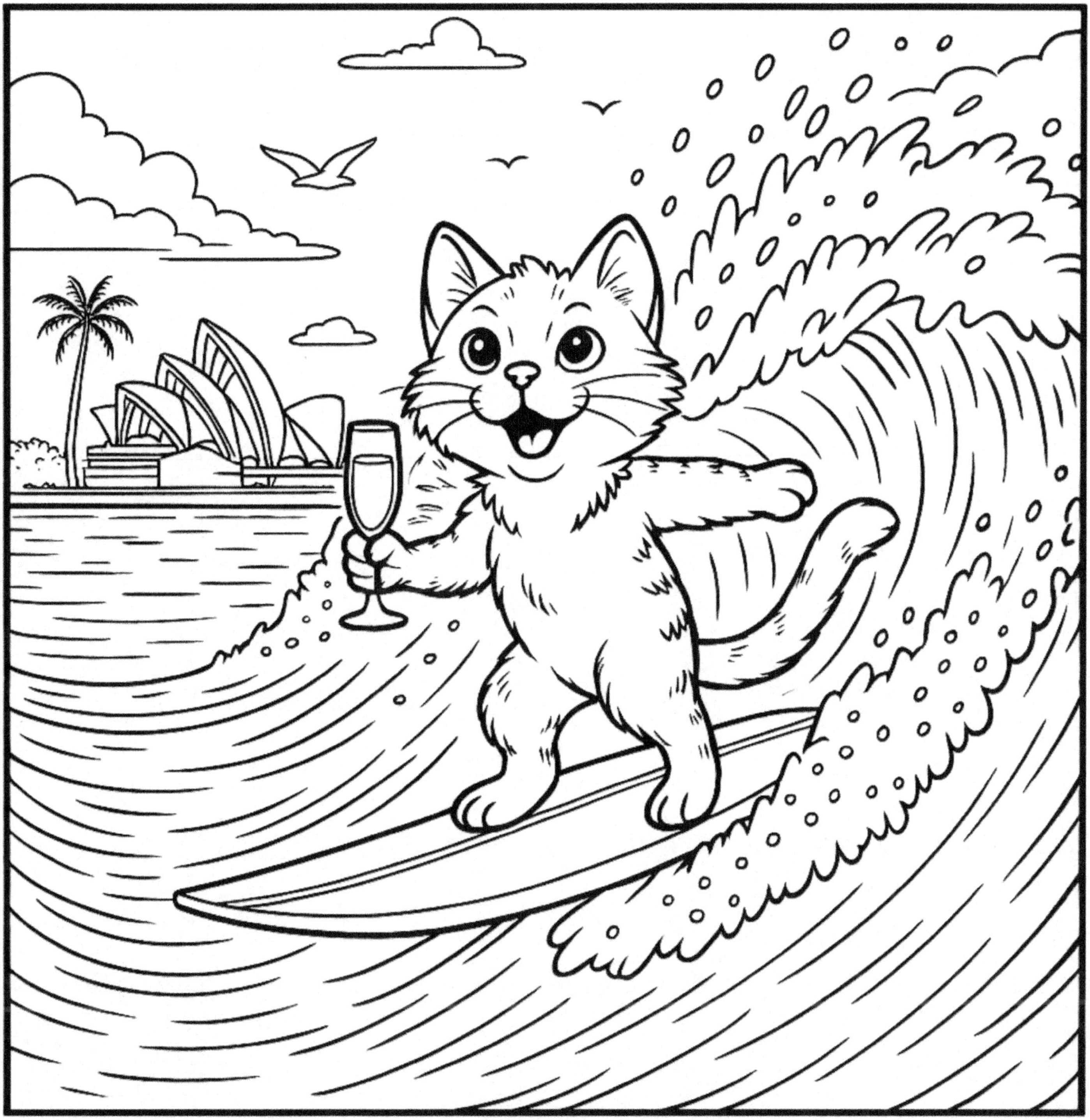

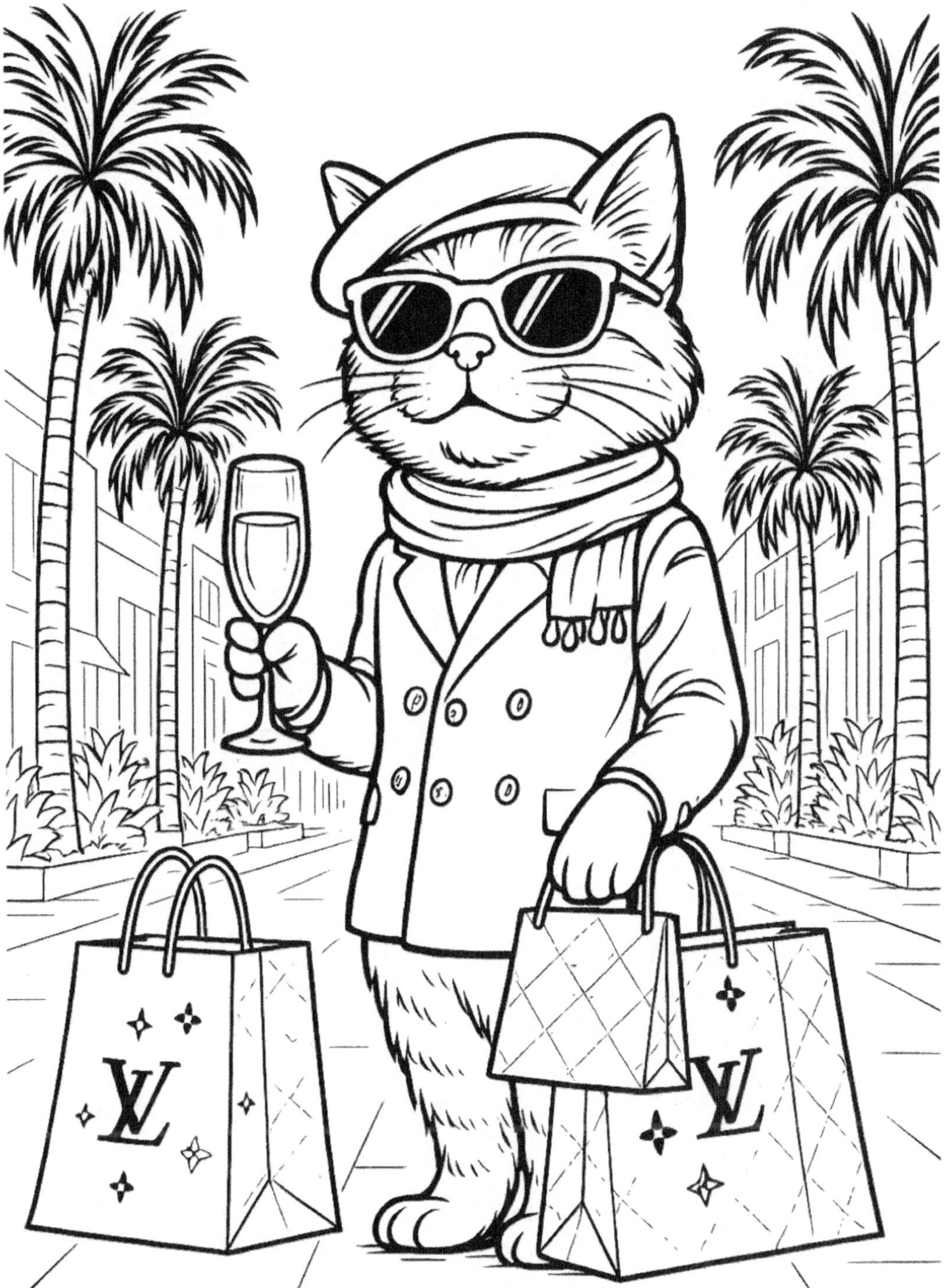

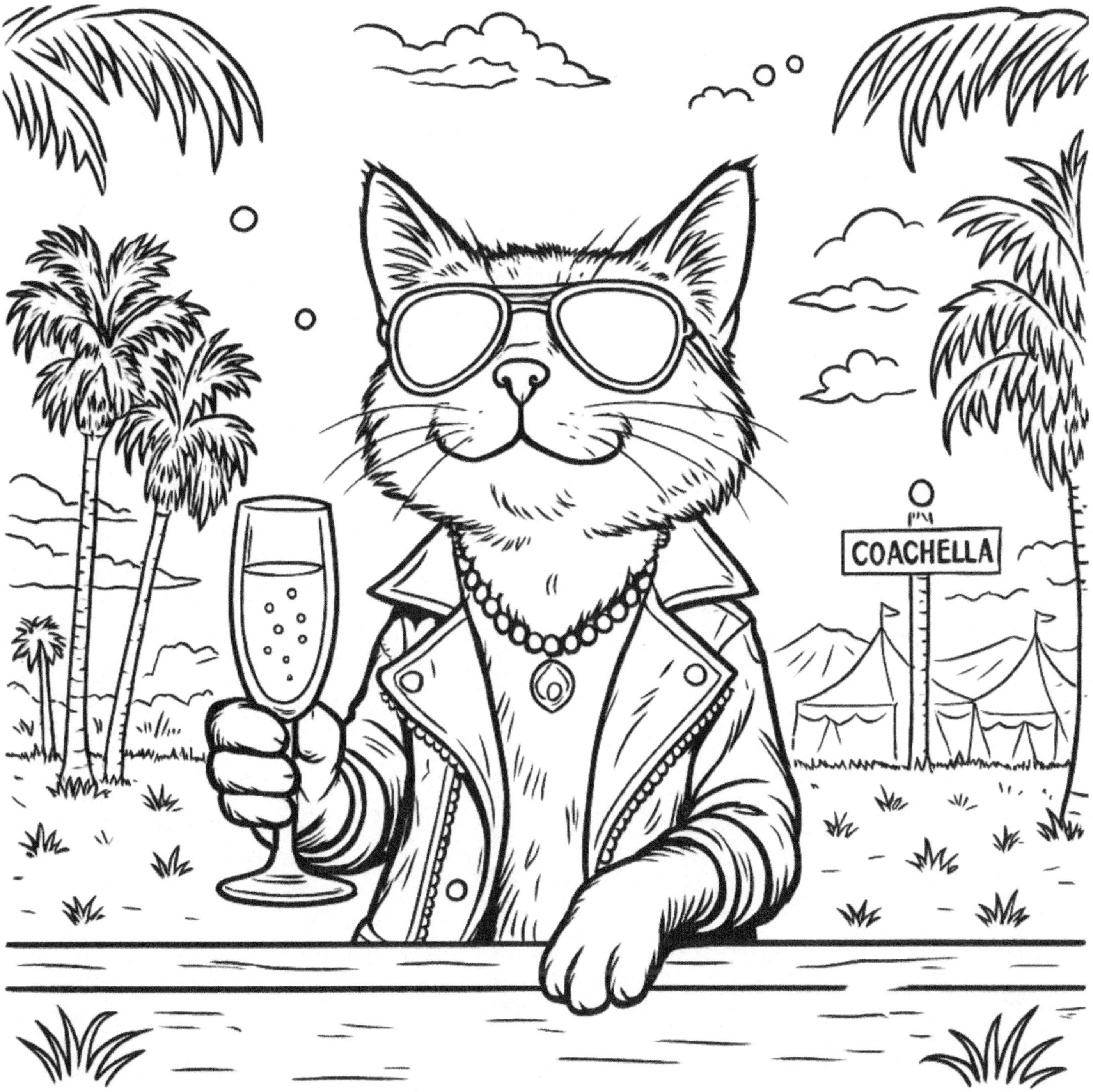
COACHELLA

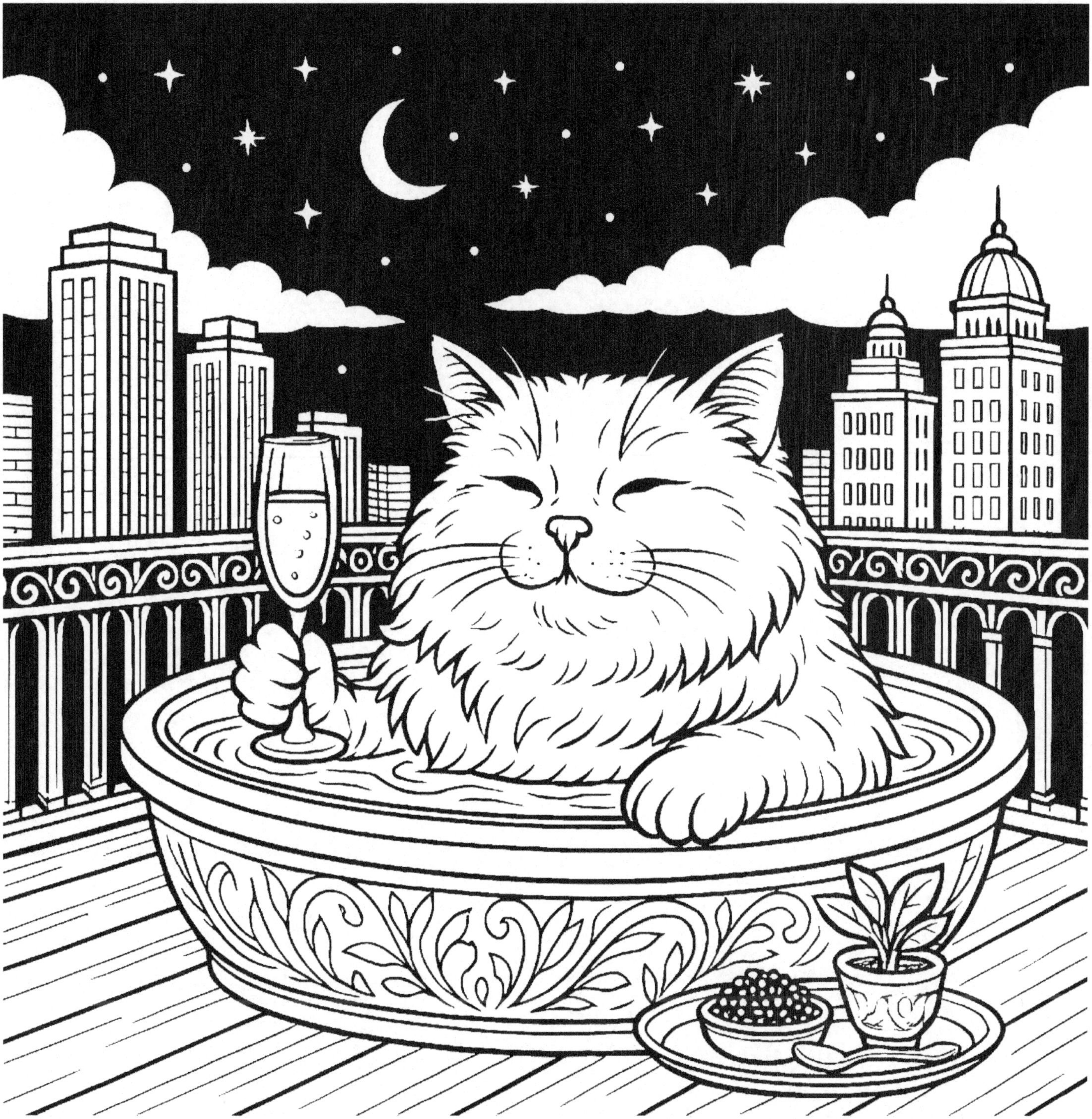

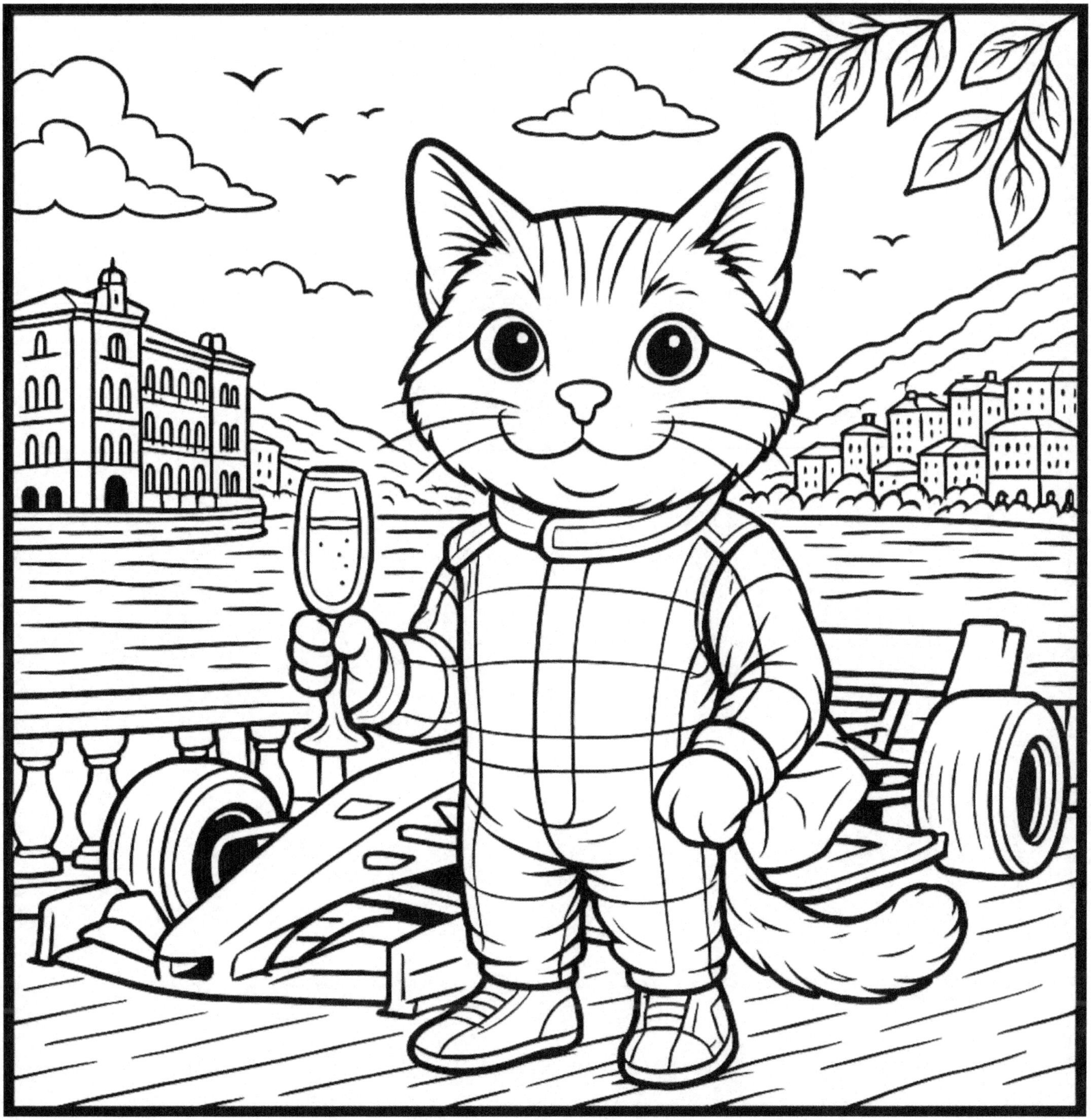

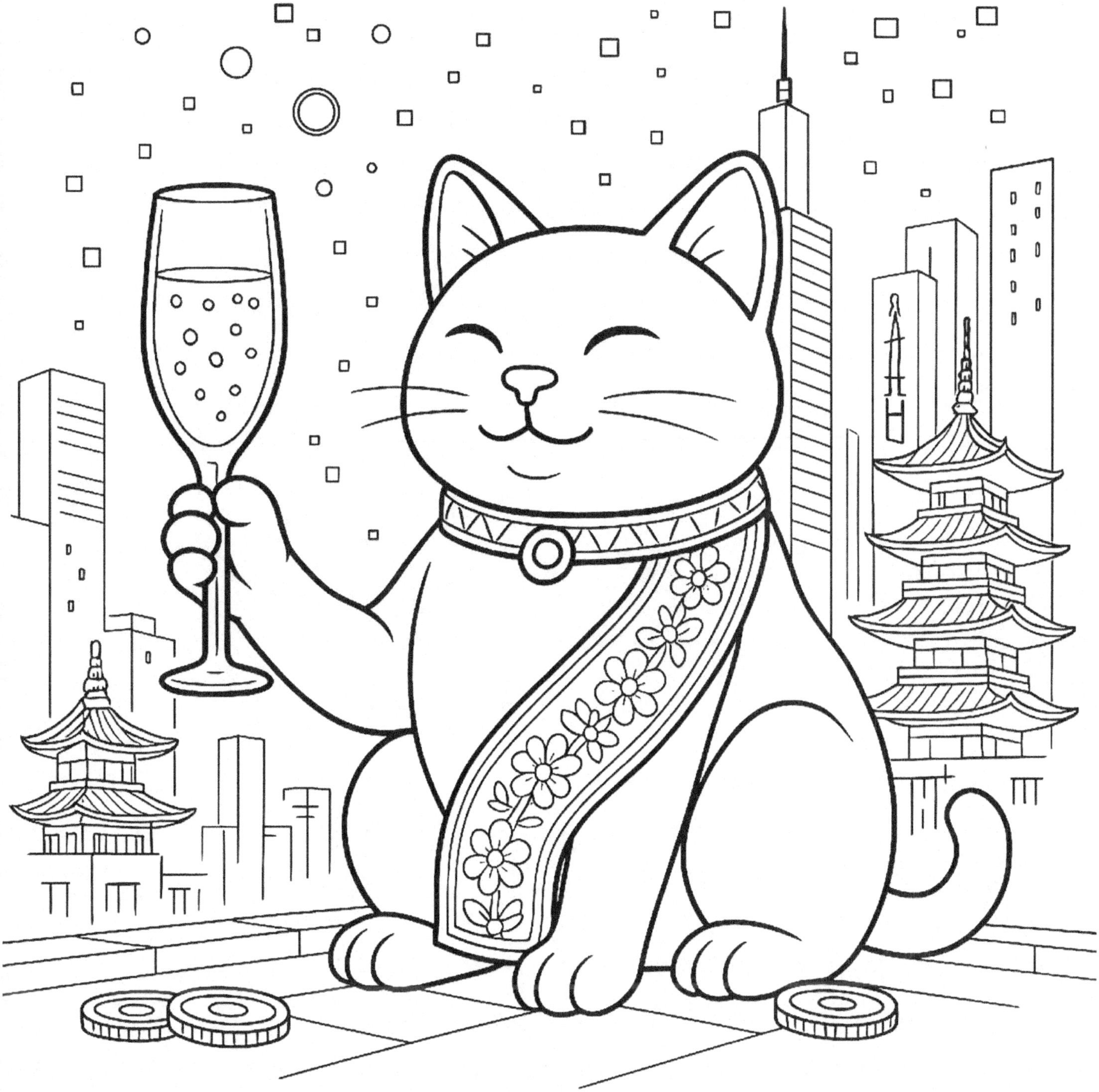

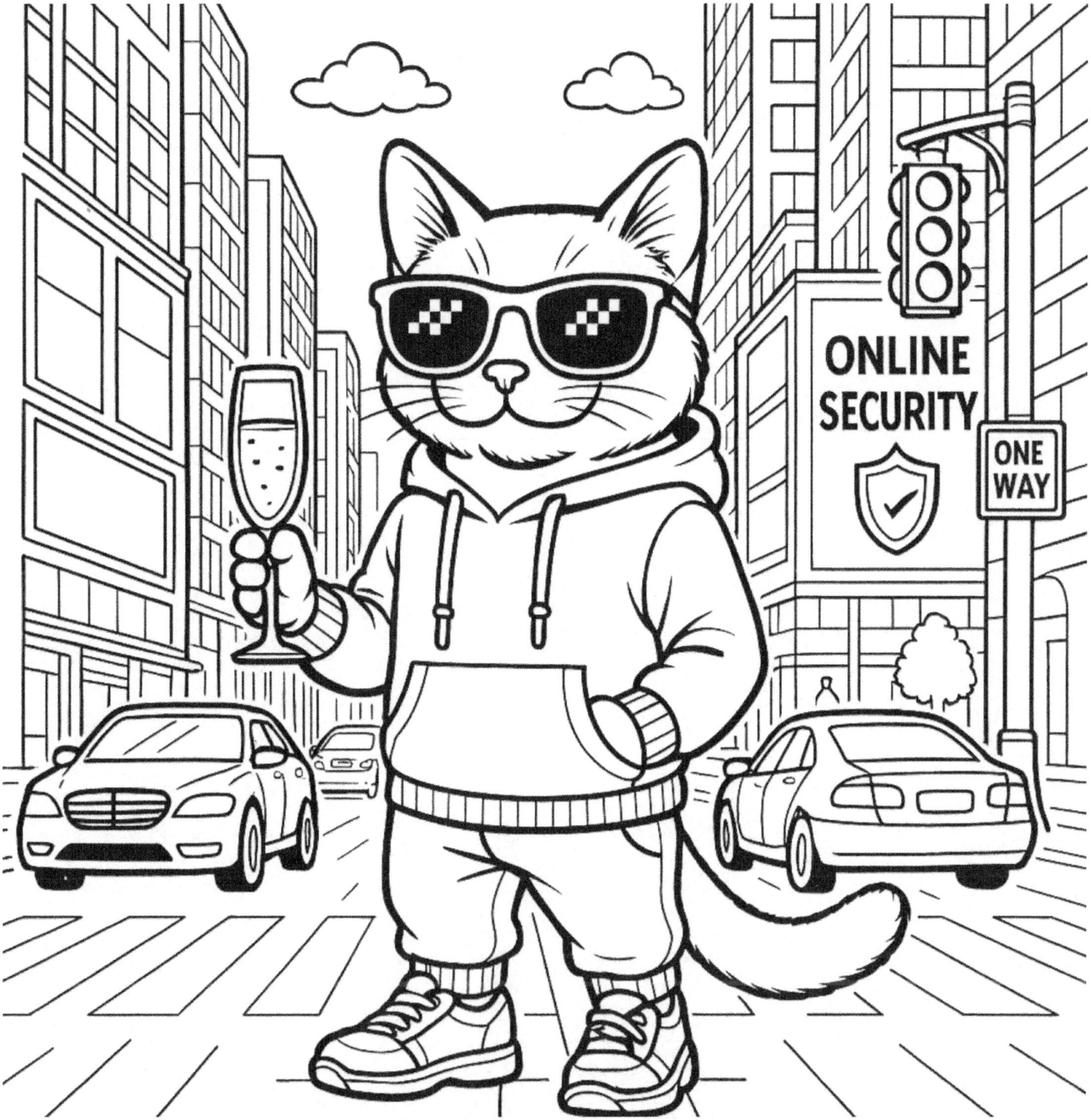
ONLINE
SECURITY
ONE
WAY

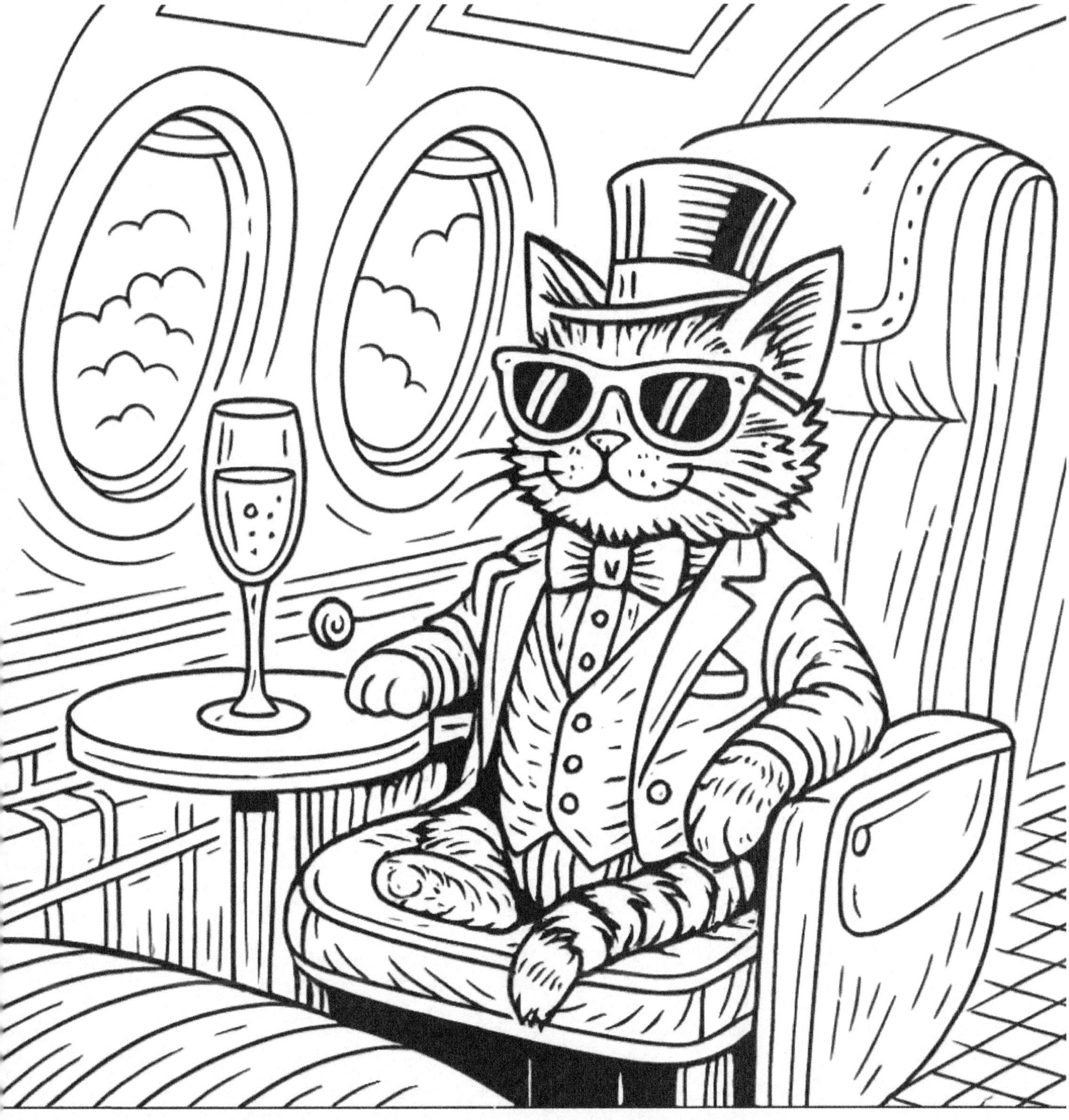

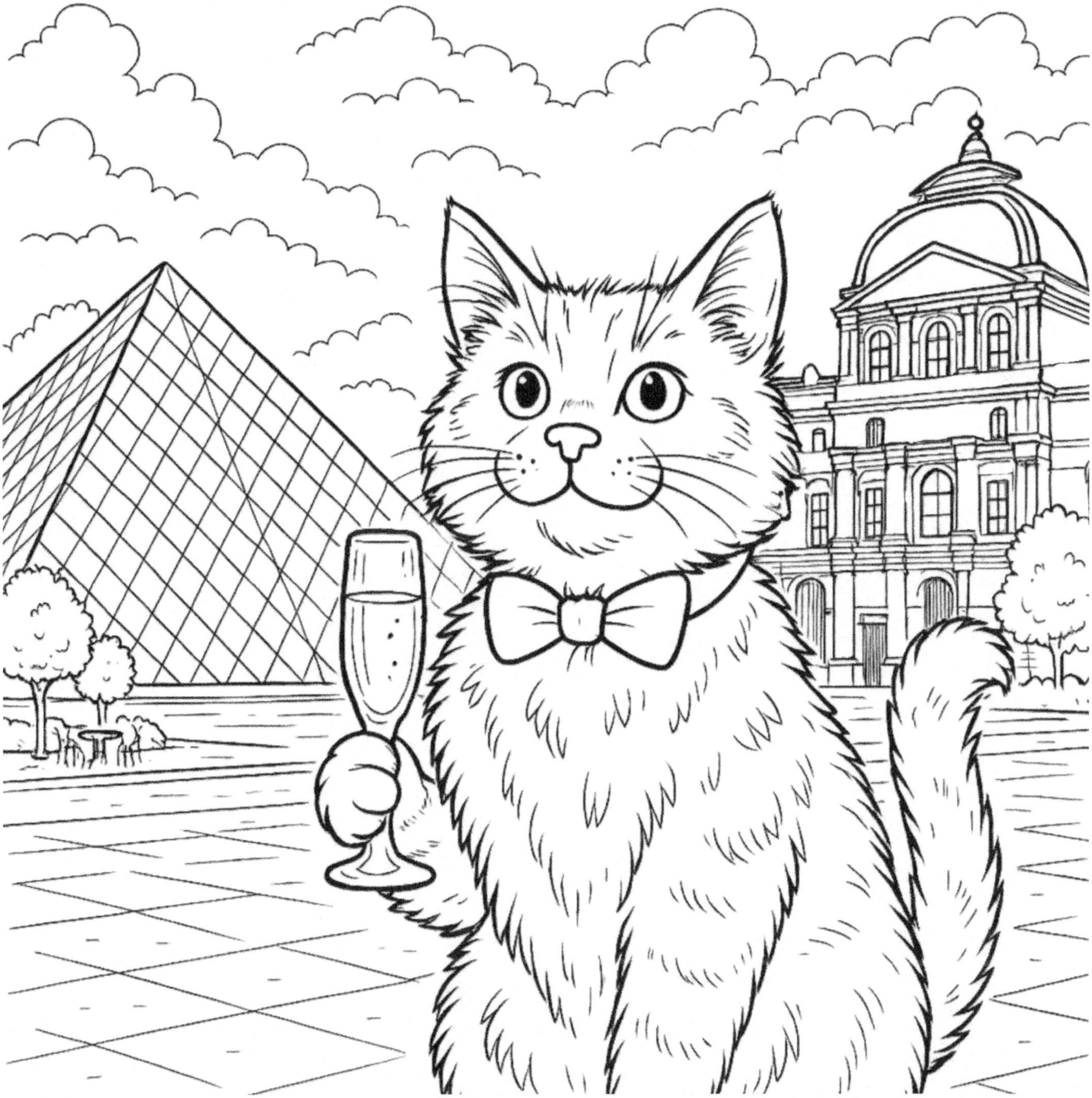

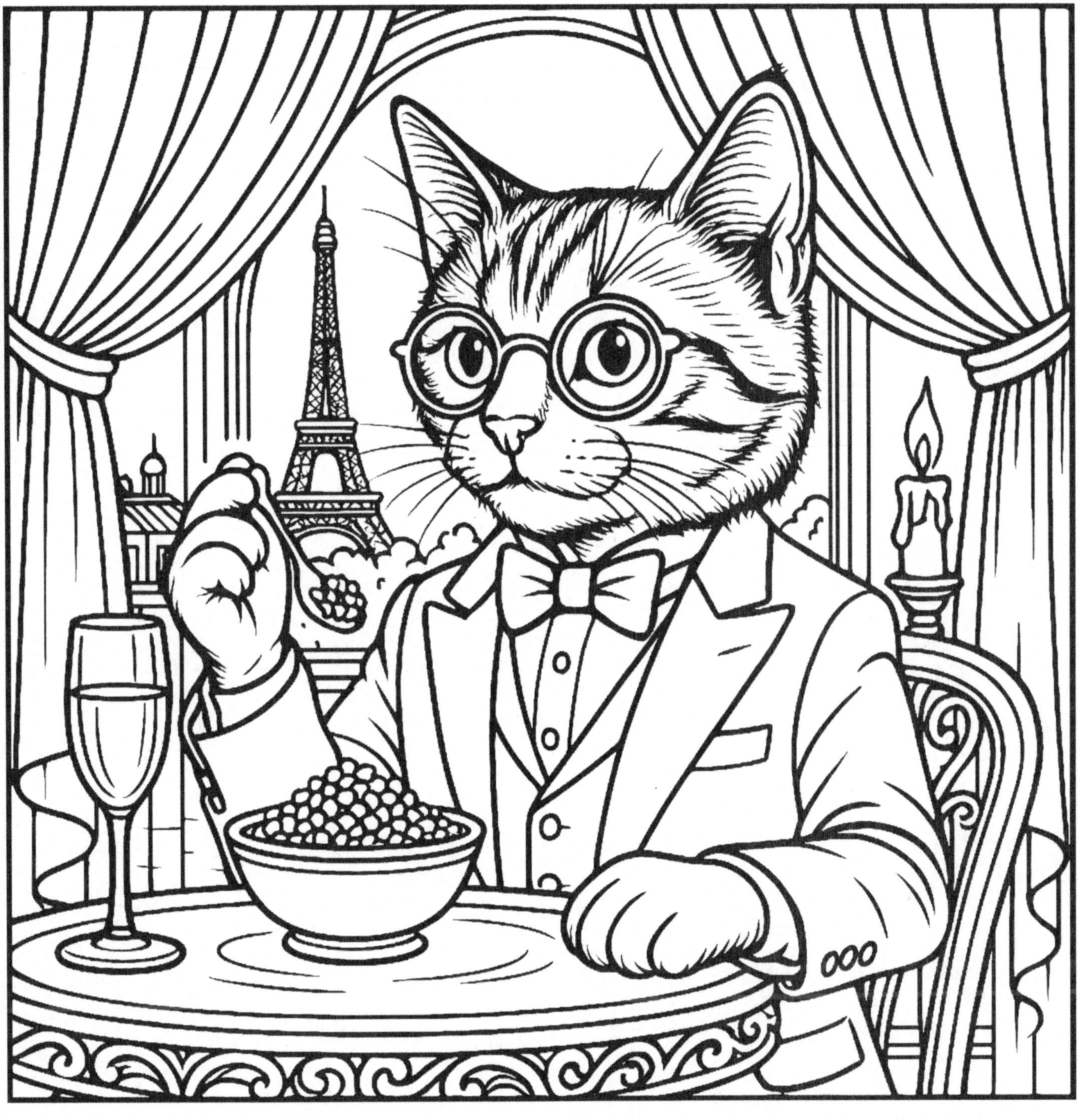

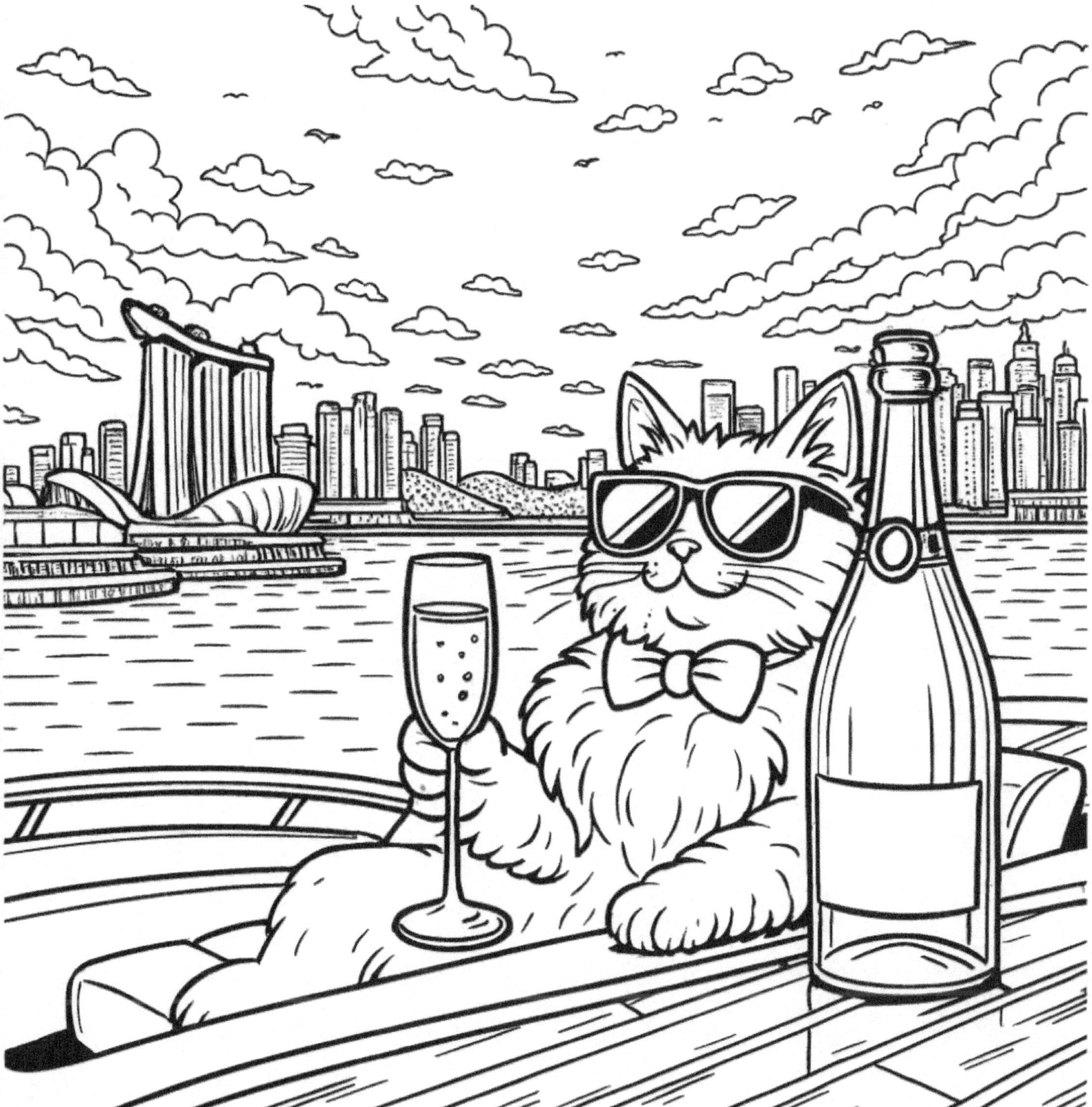

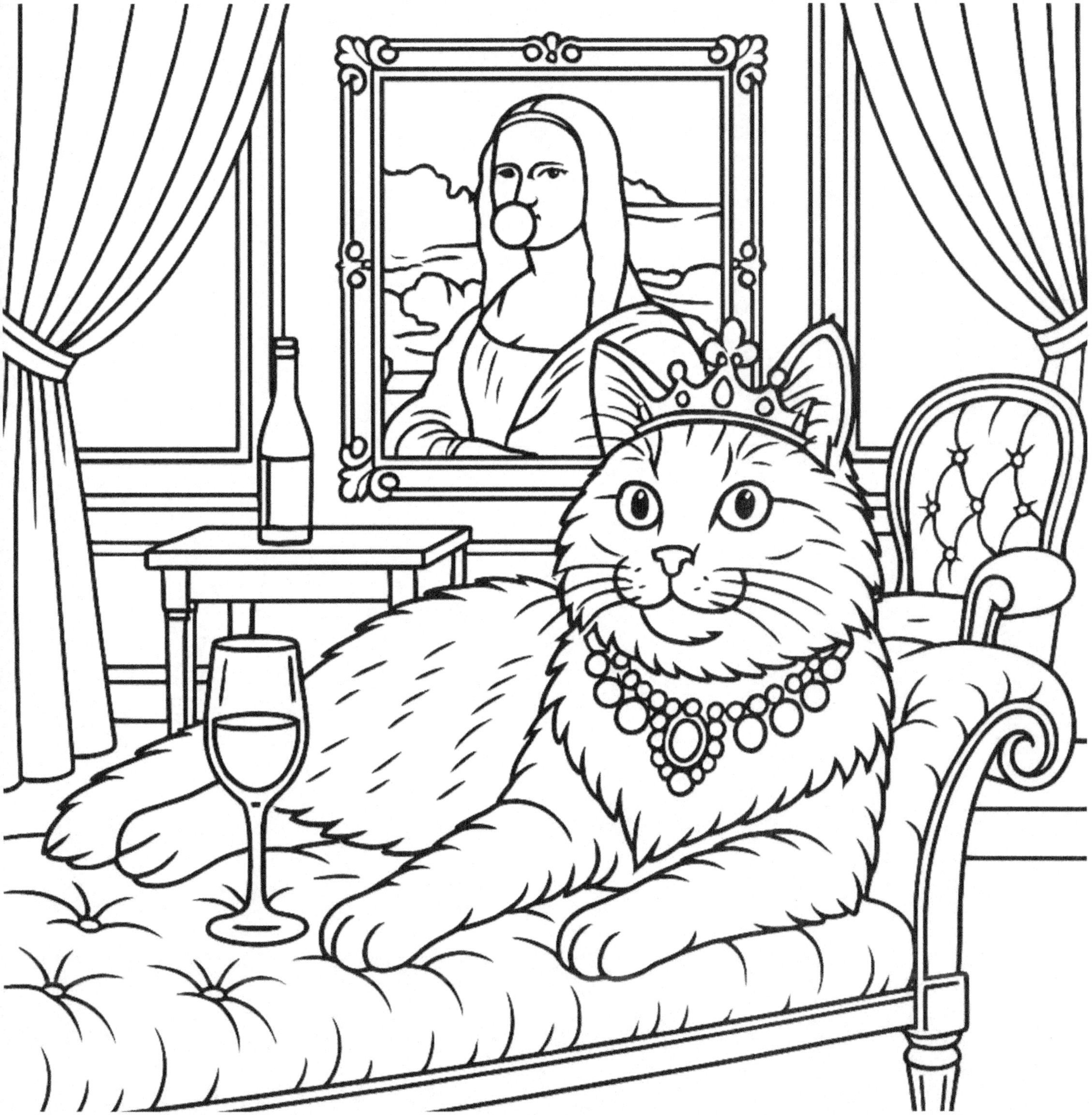

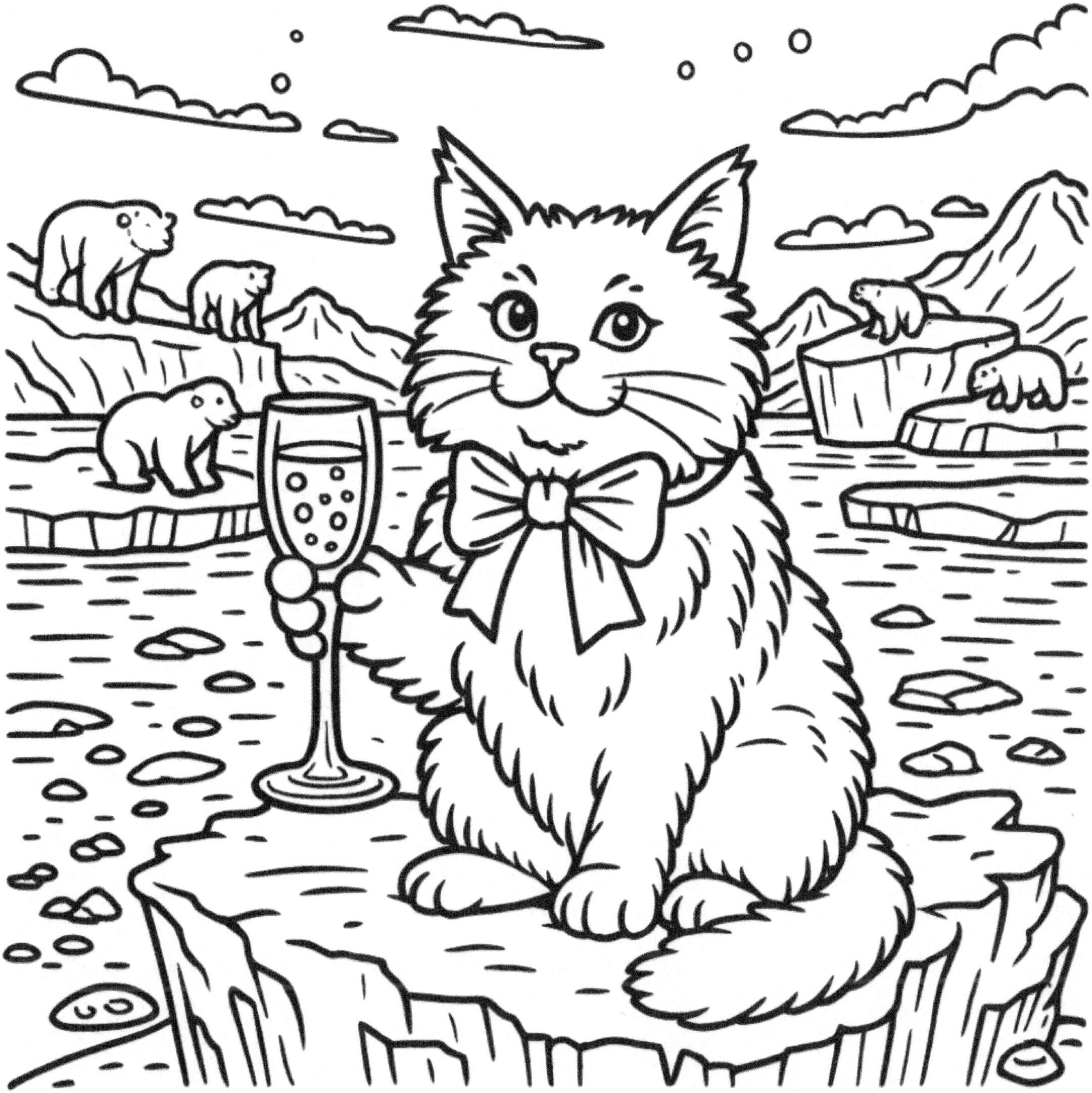

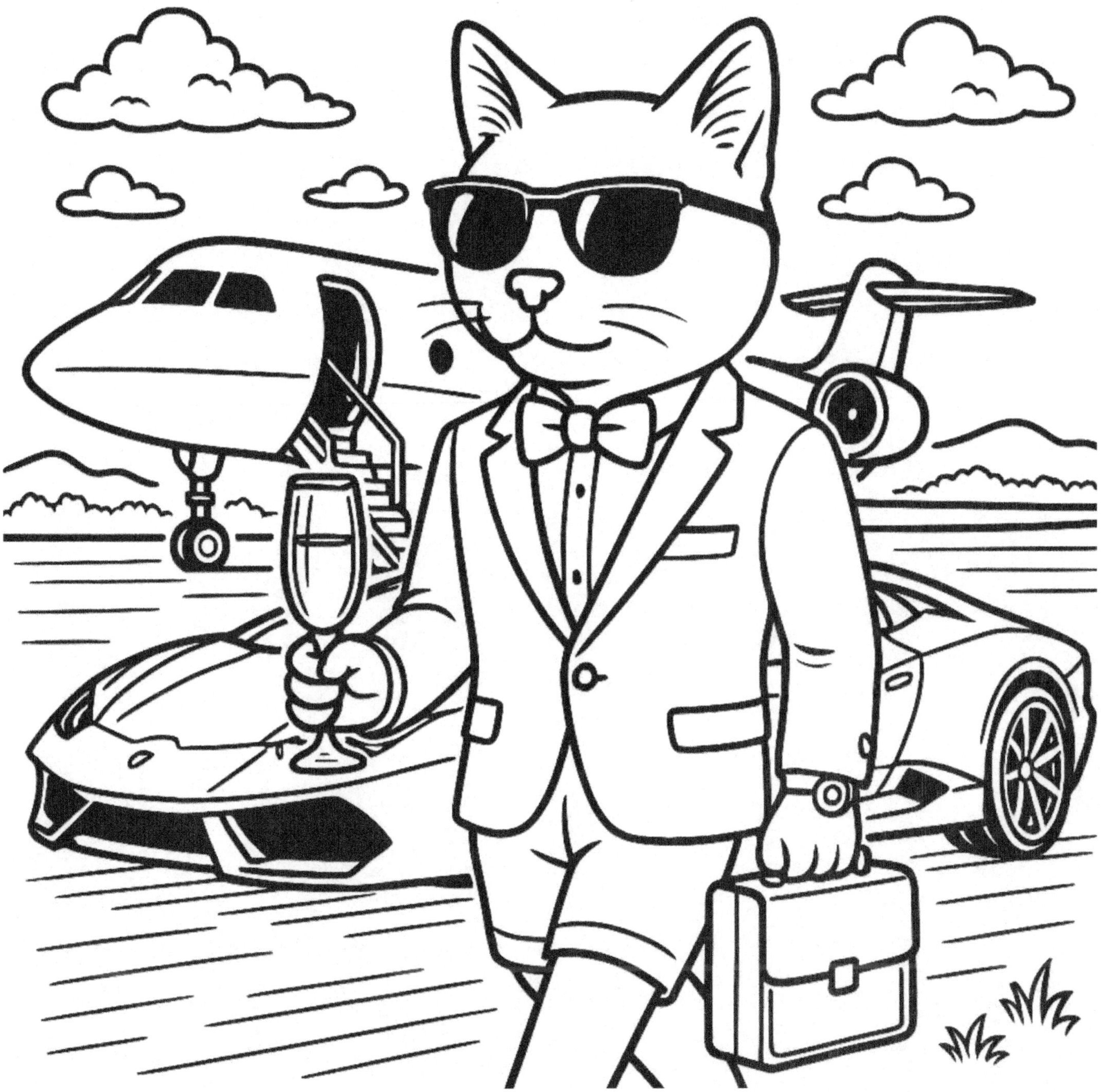

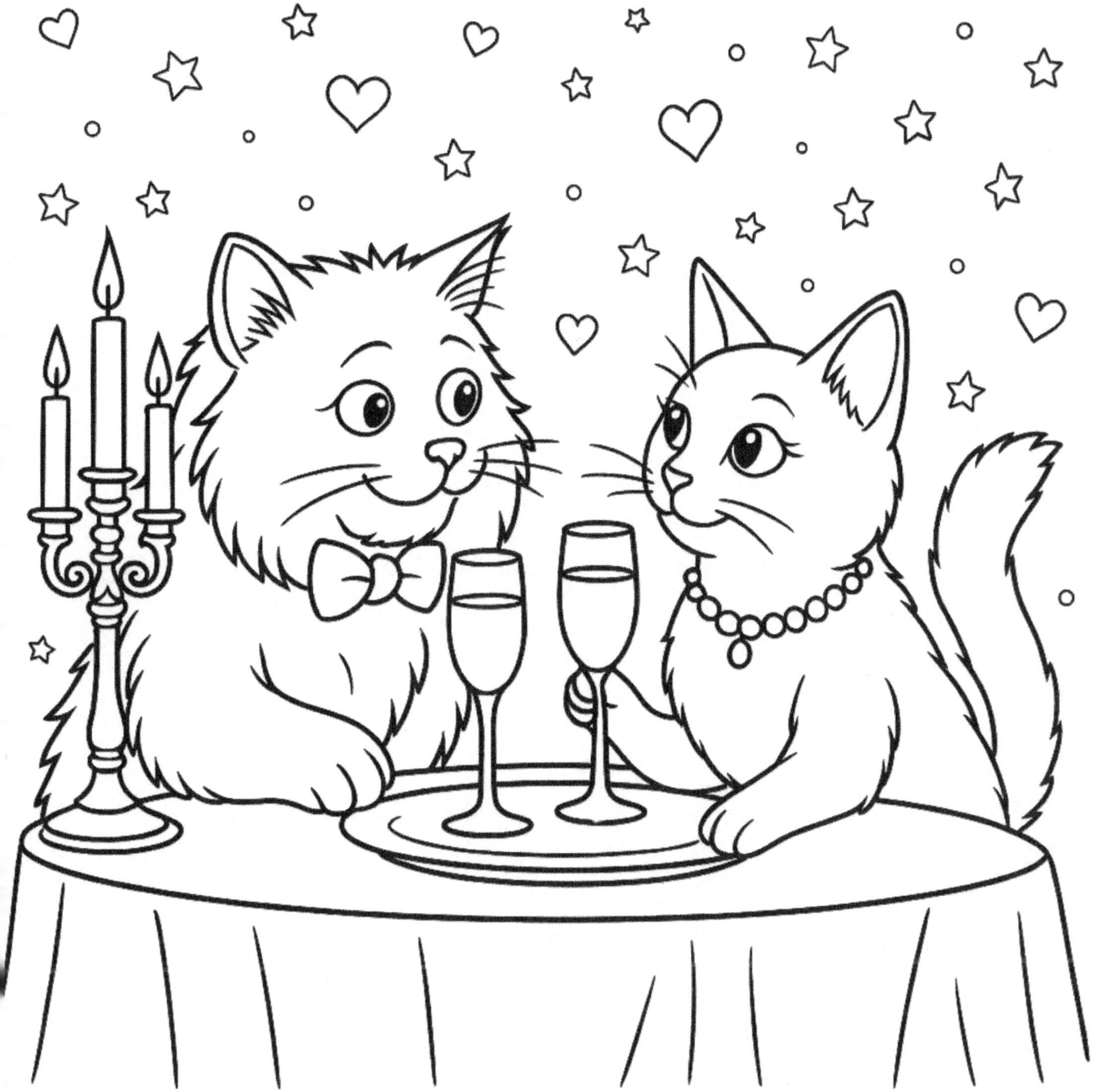

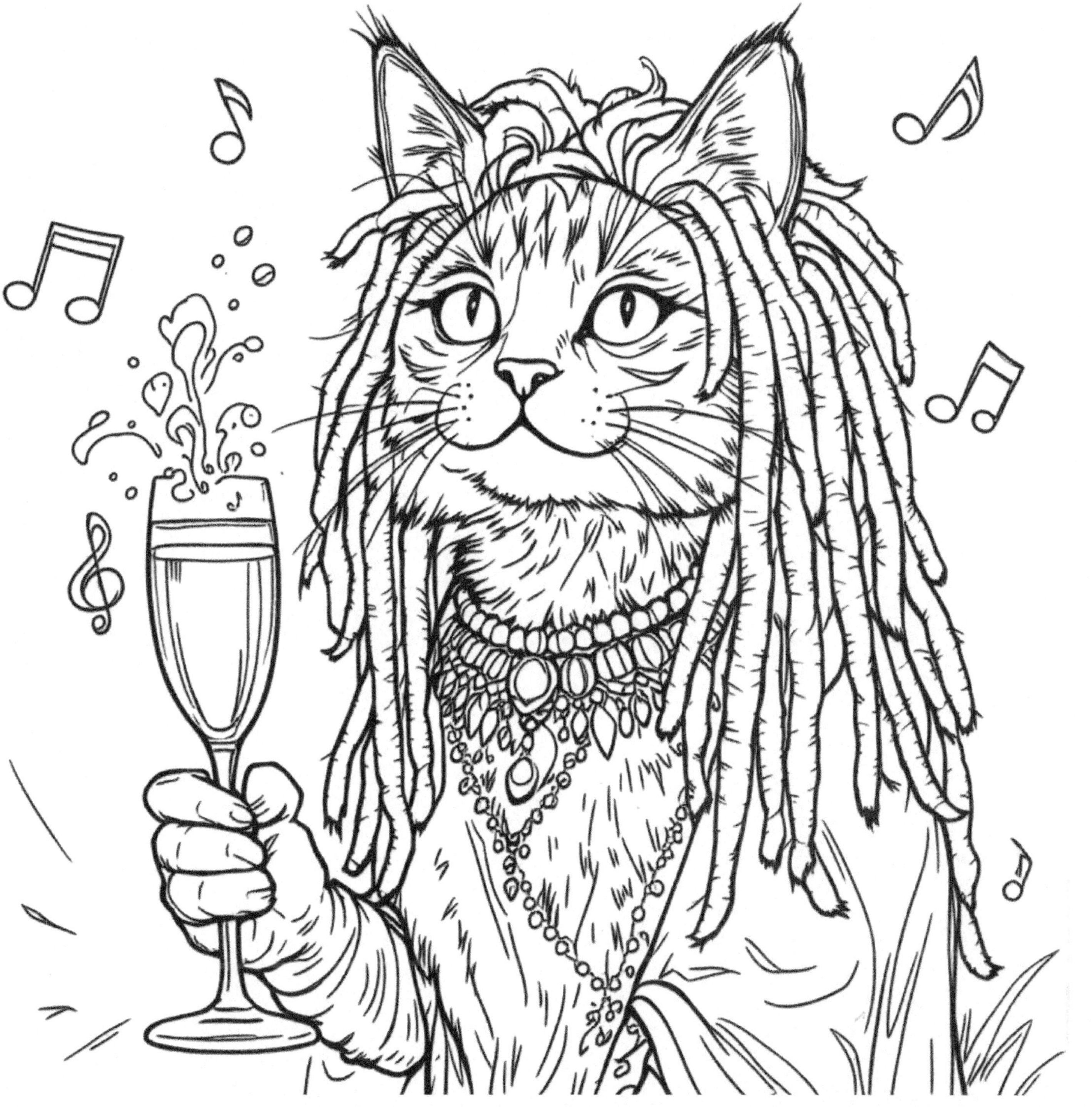

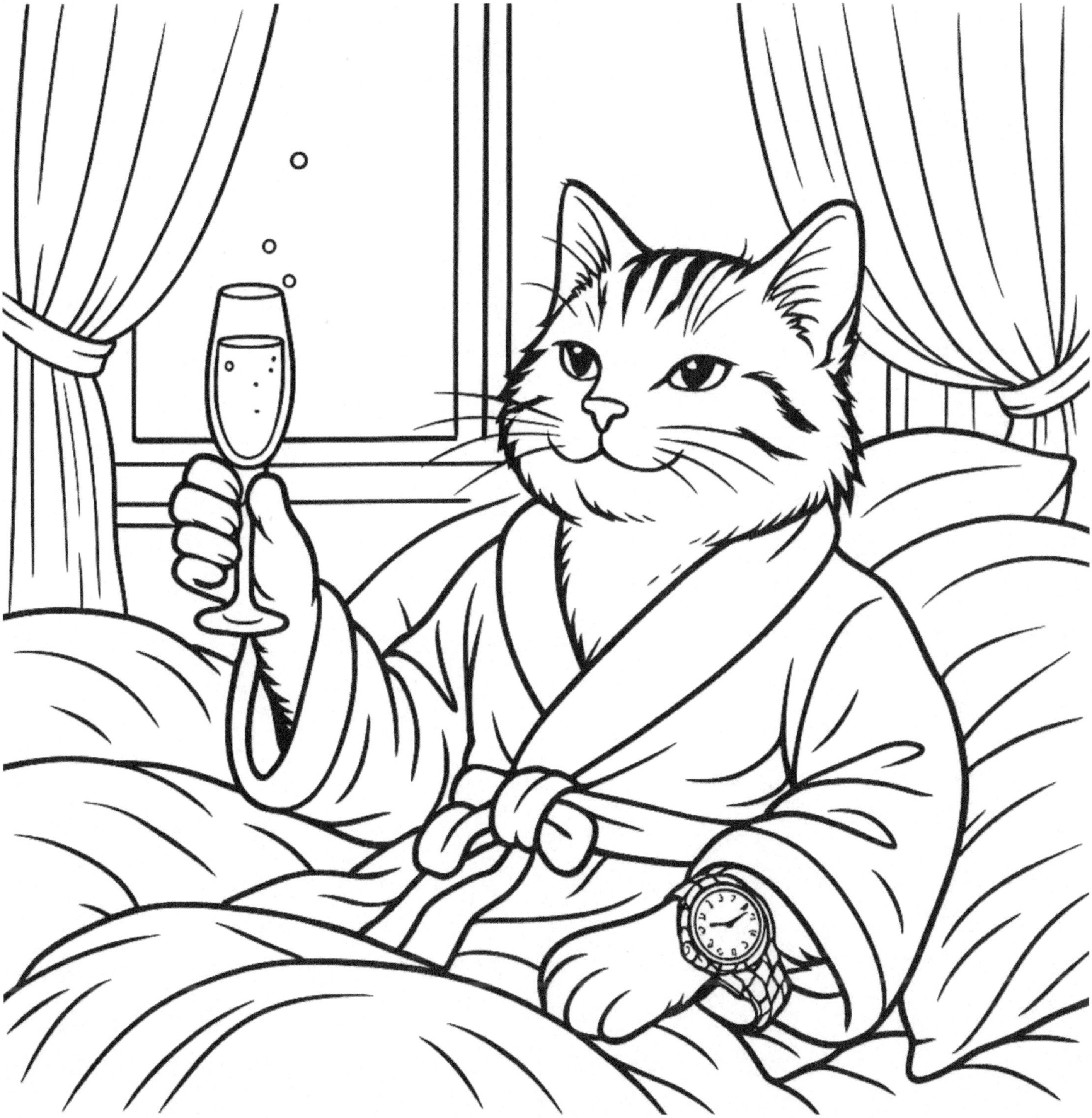

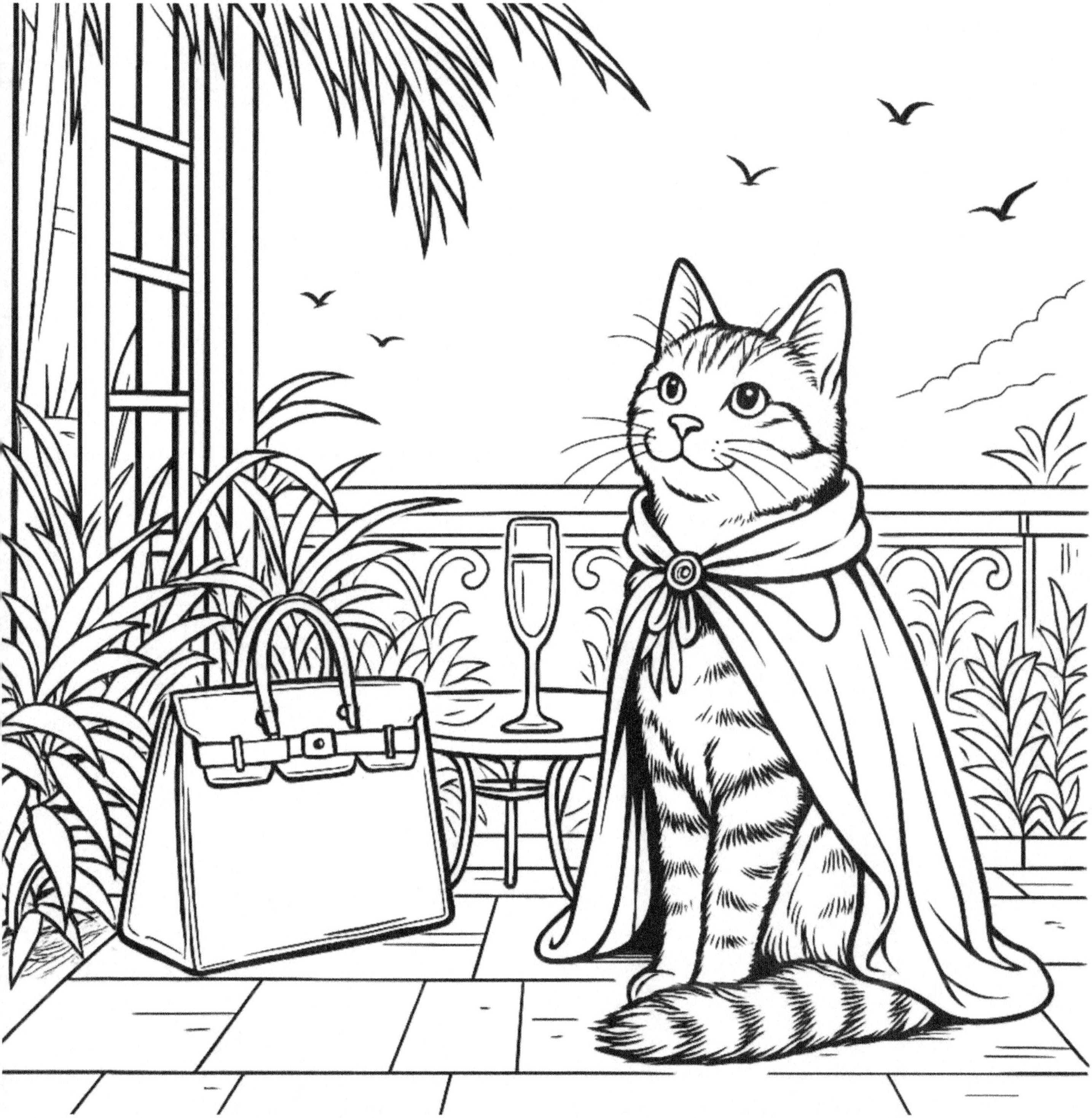

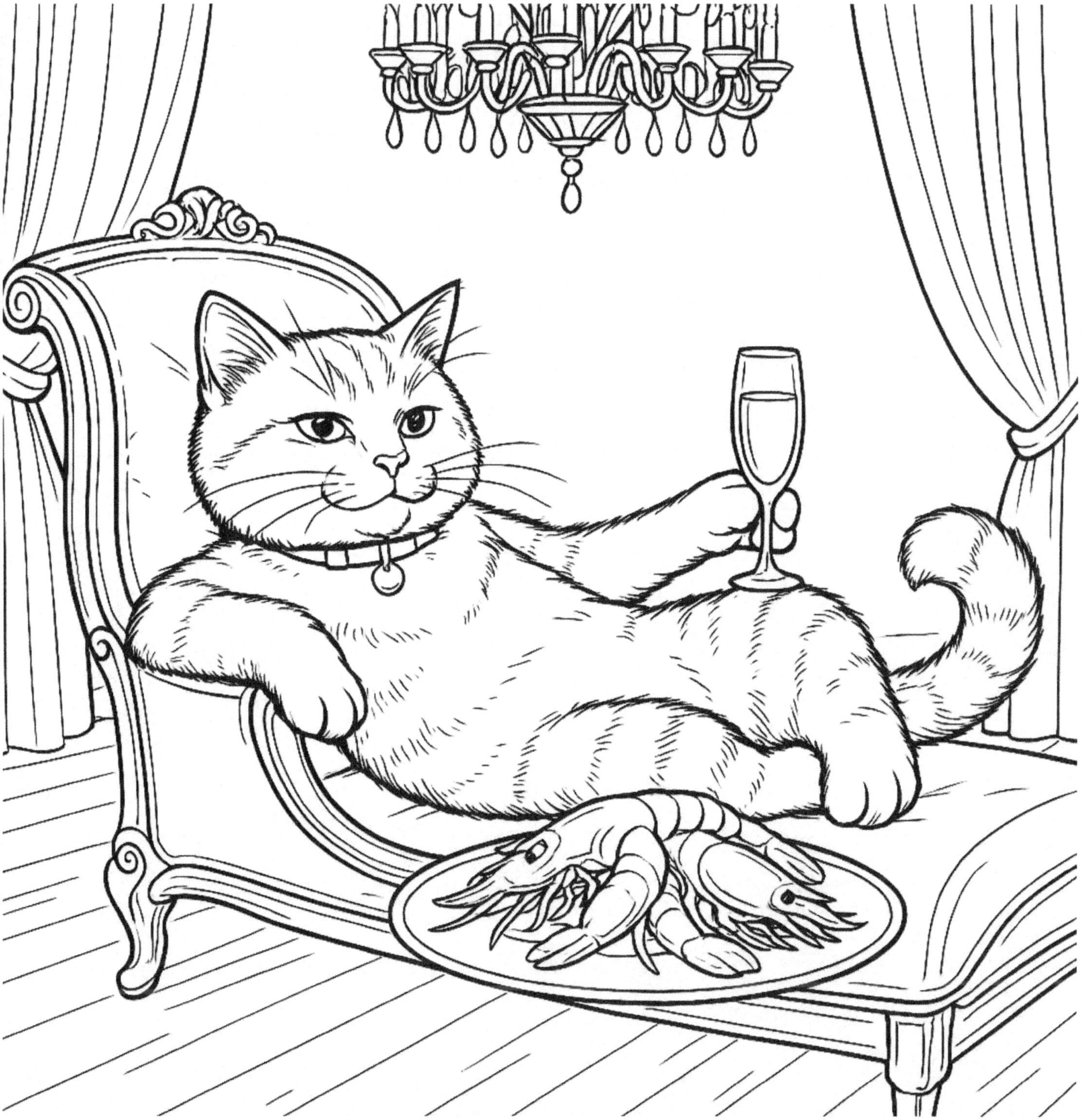

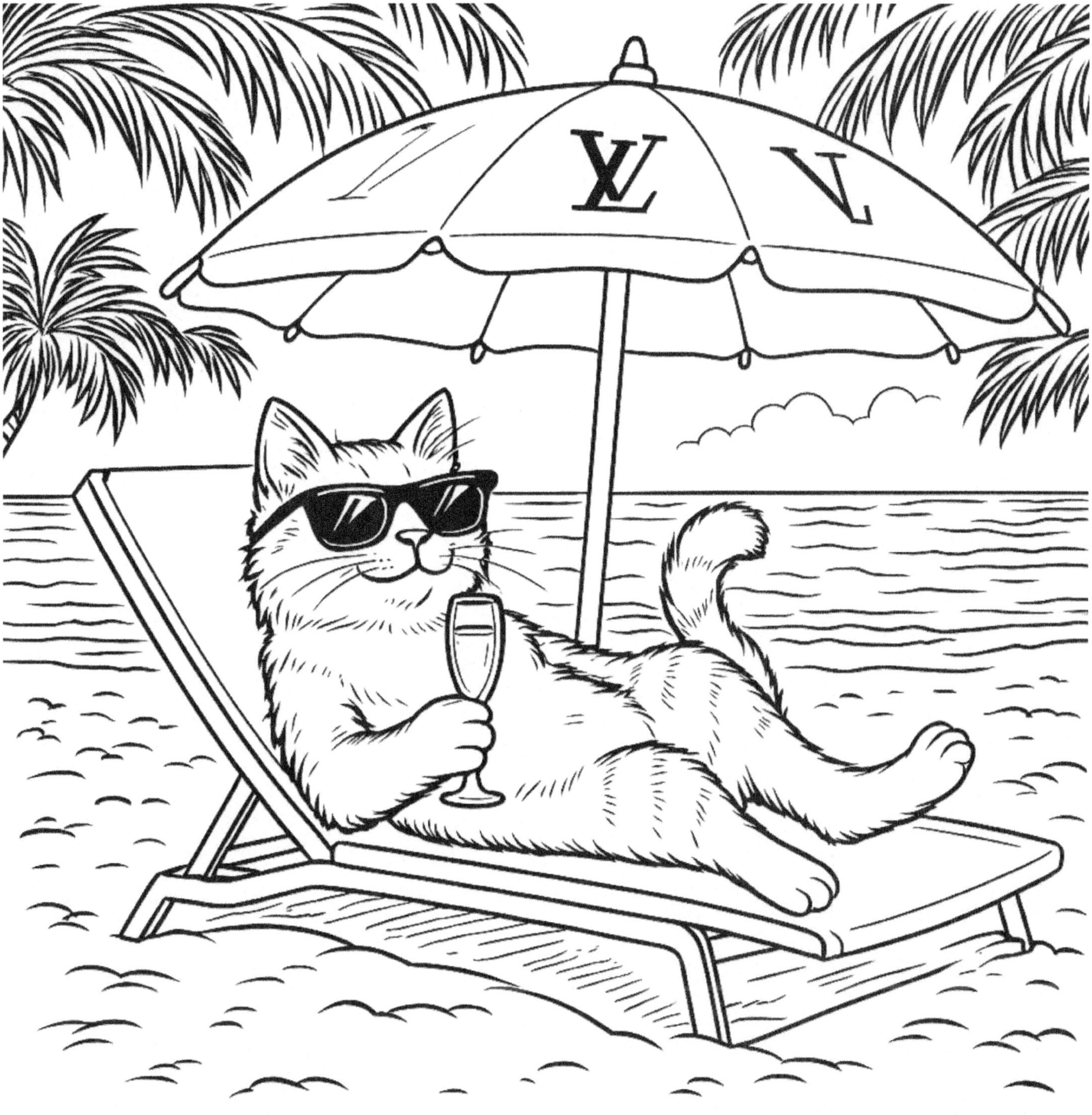

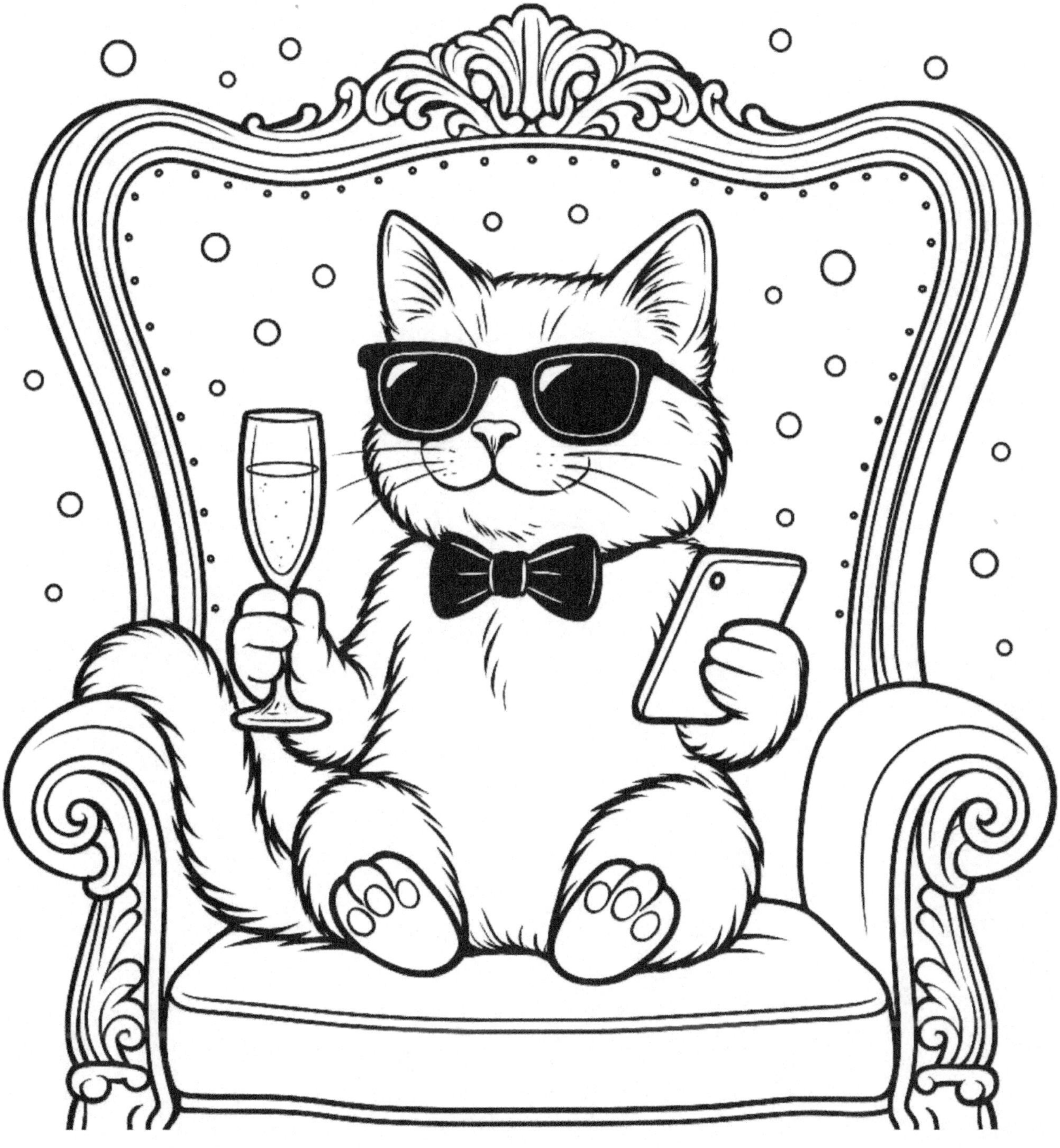

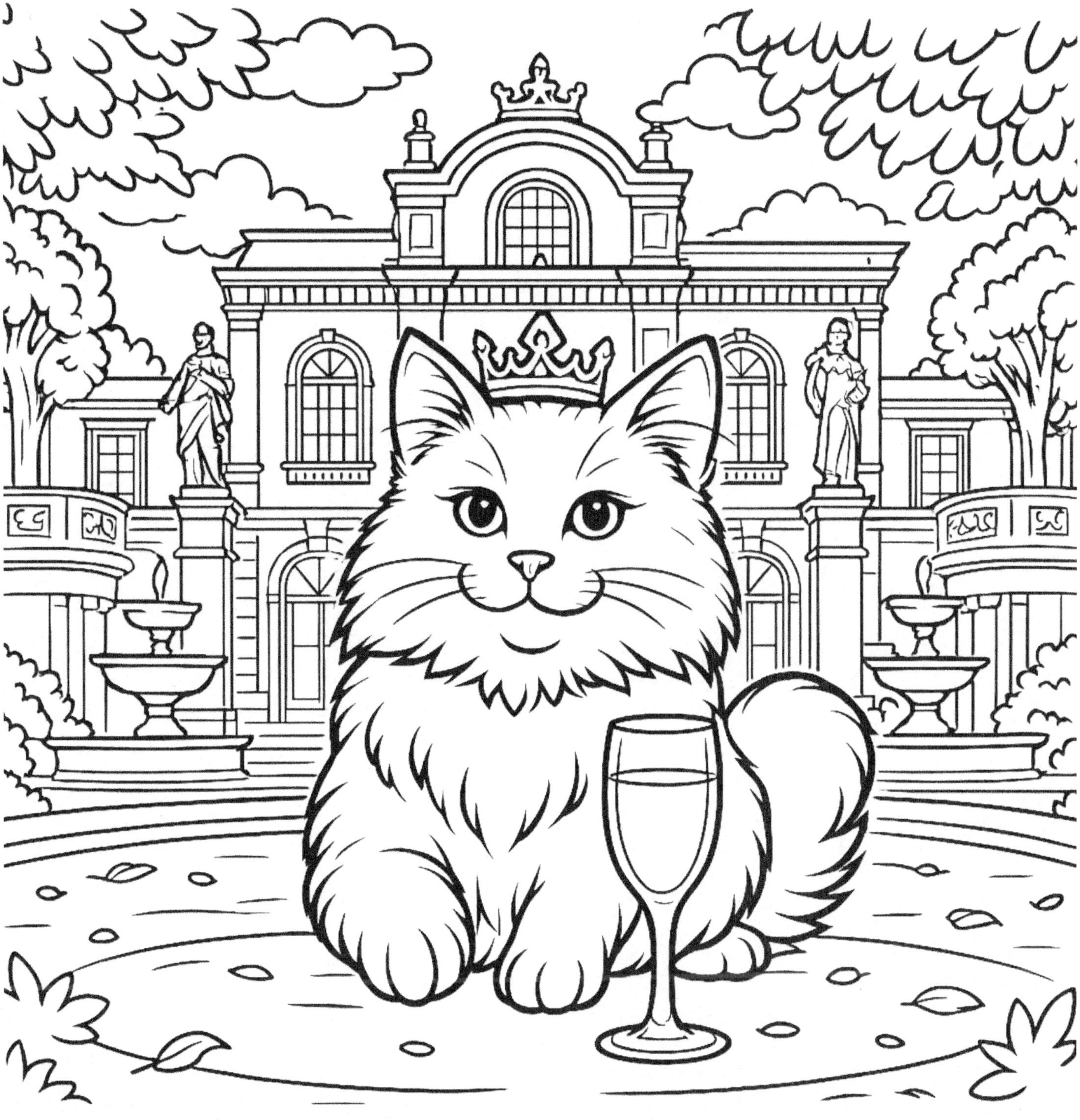

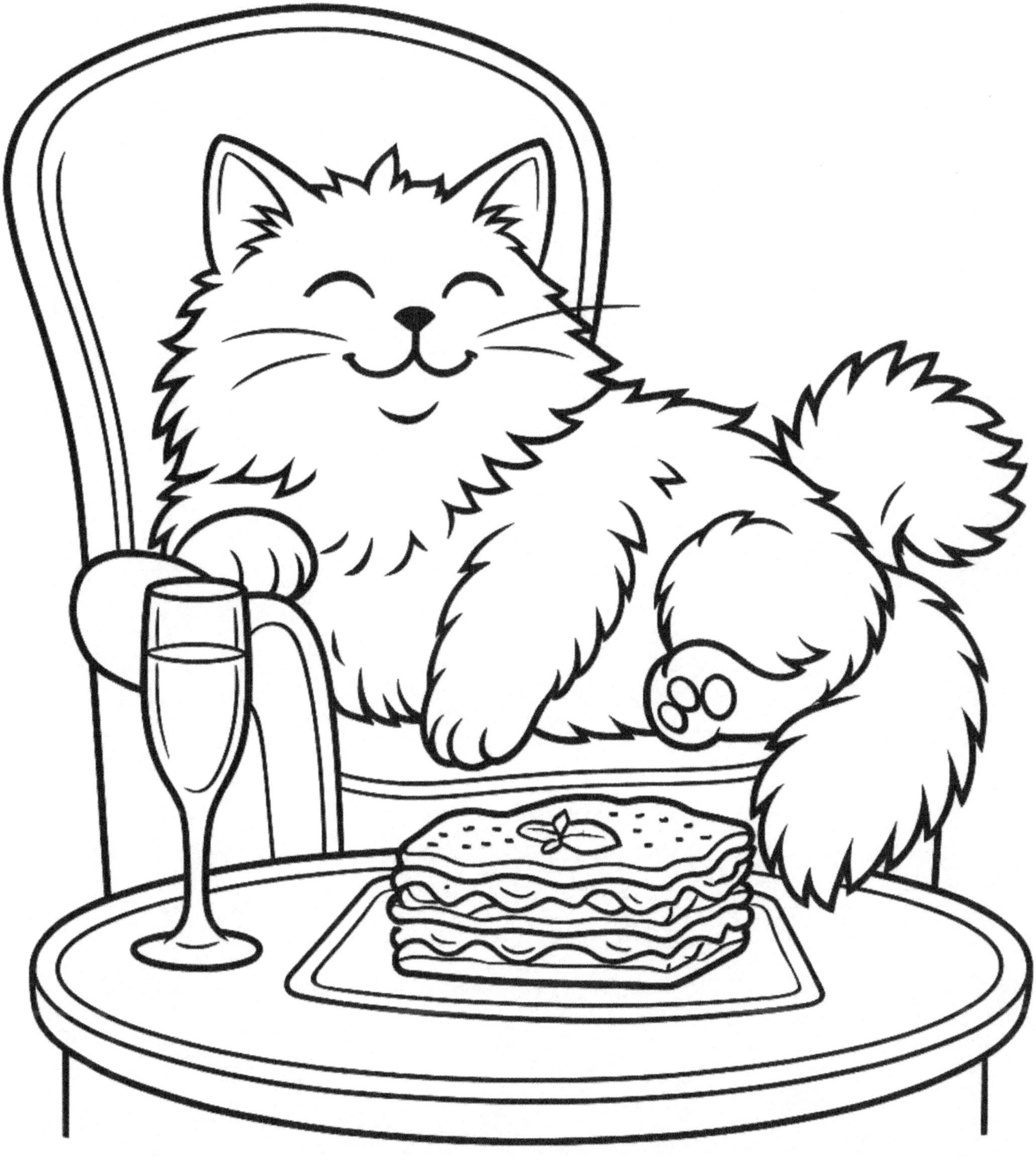

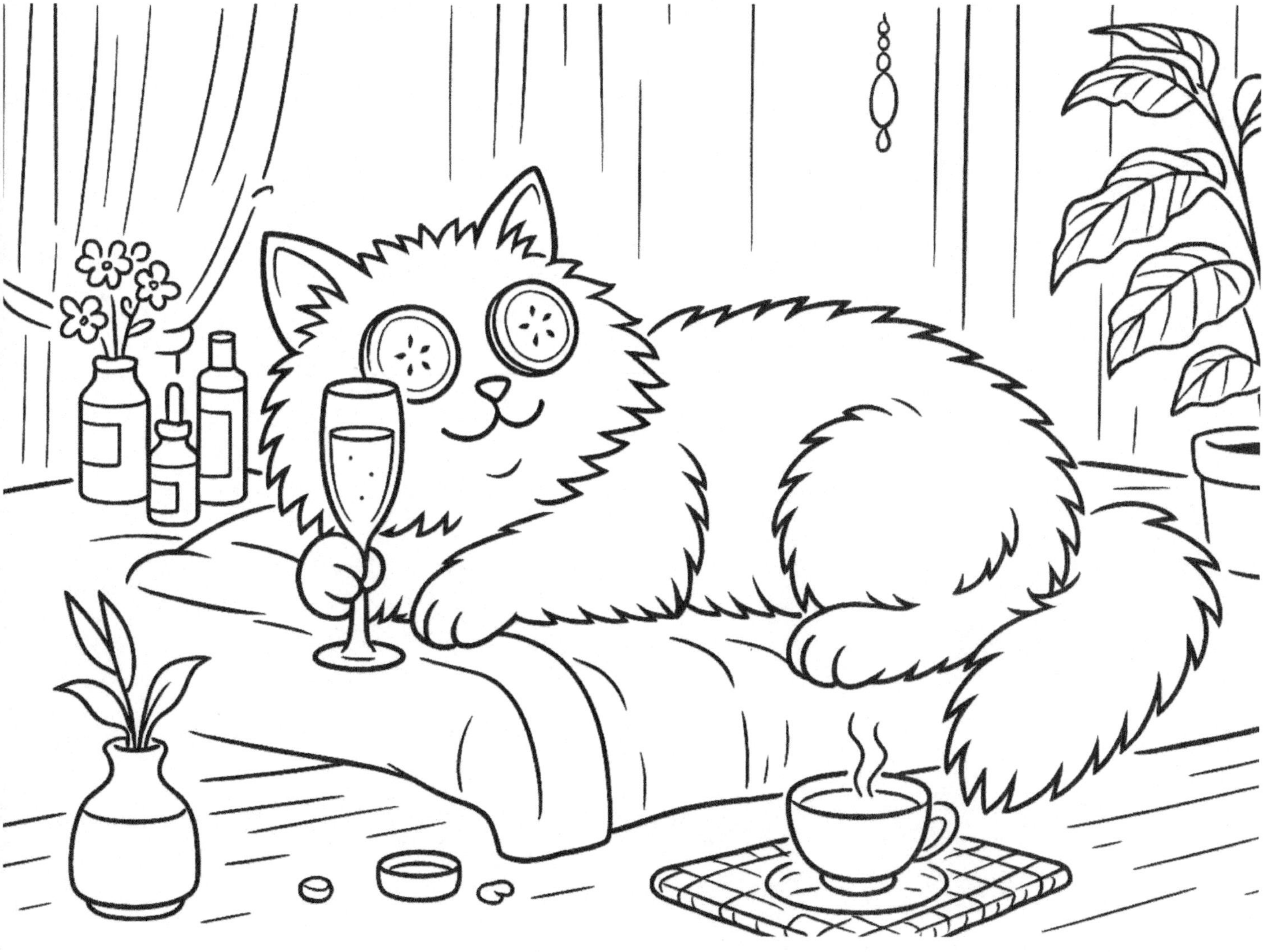

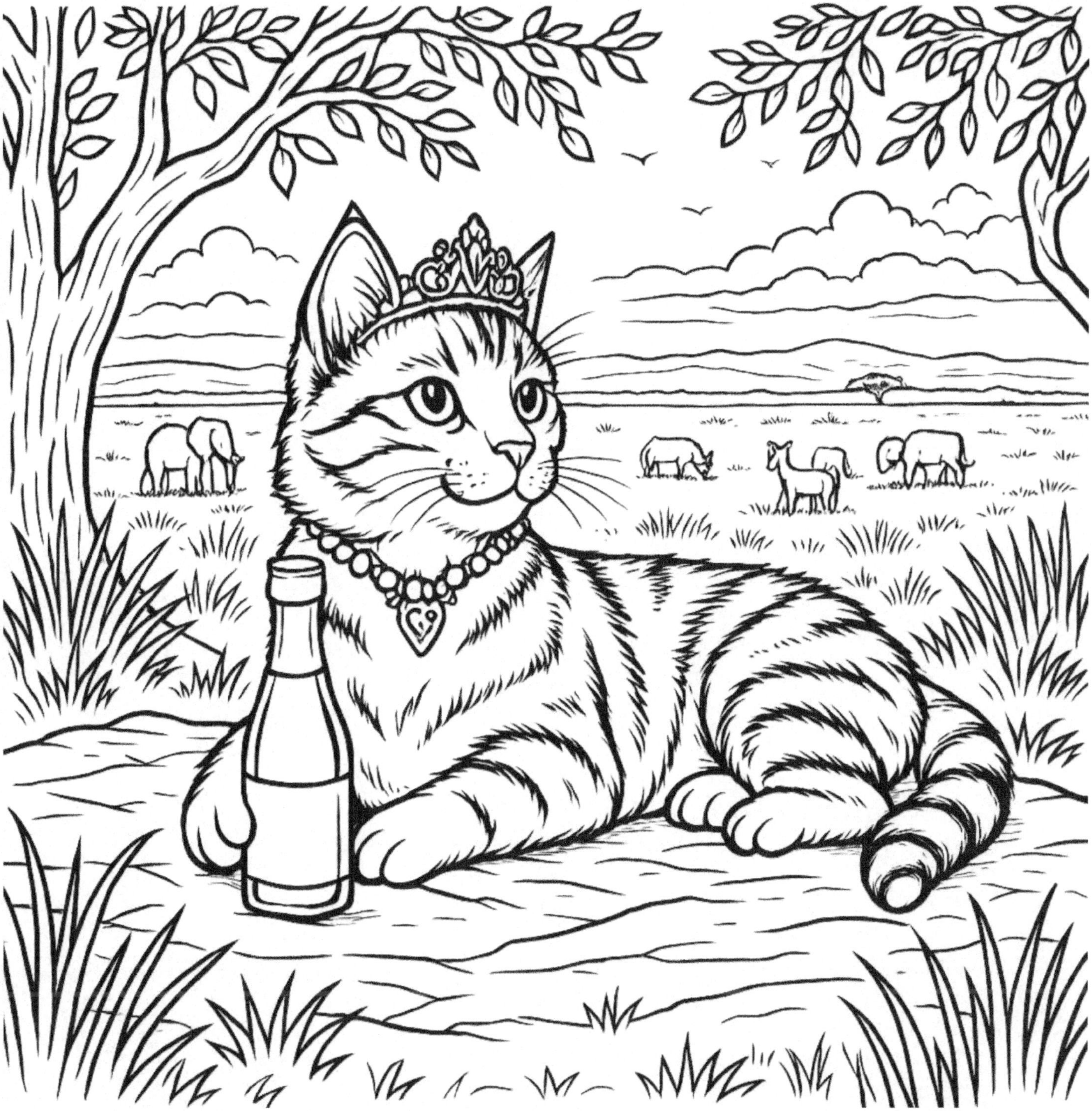

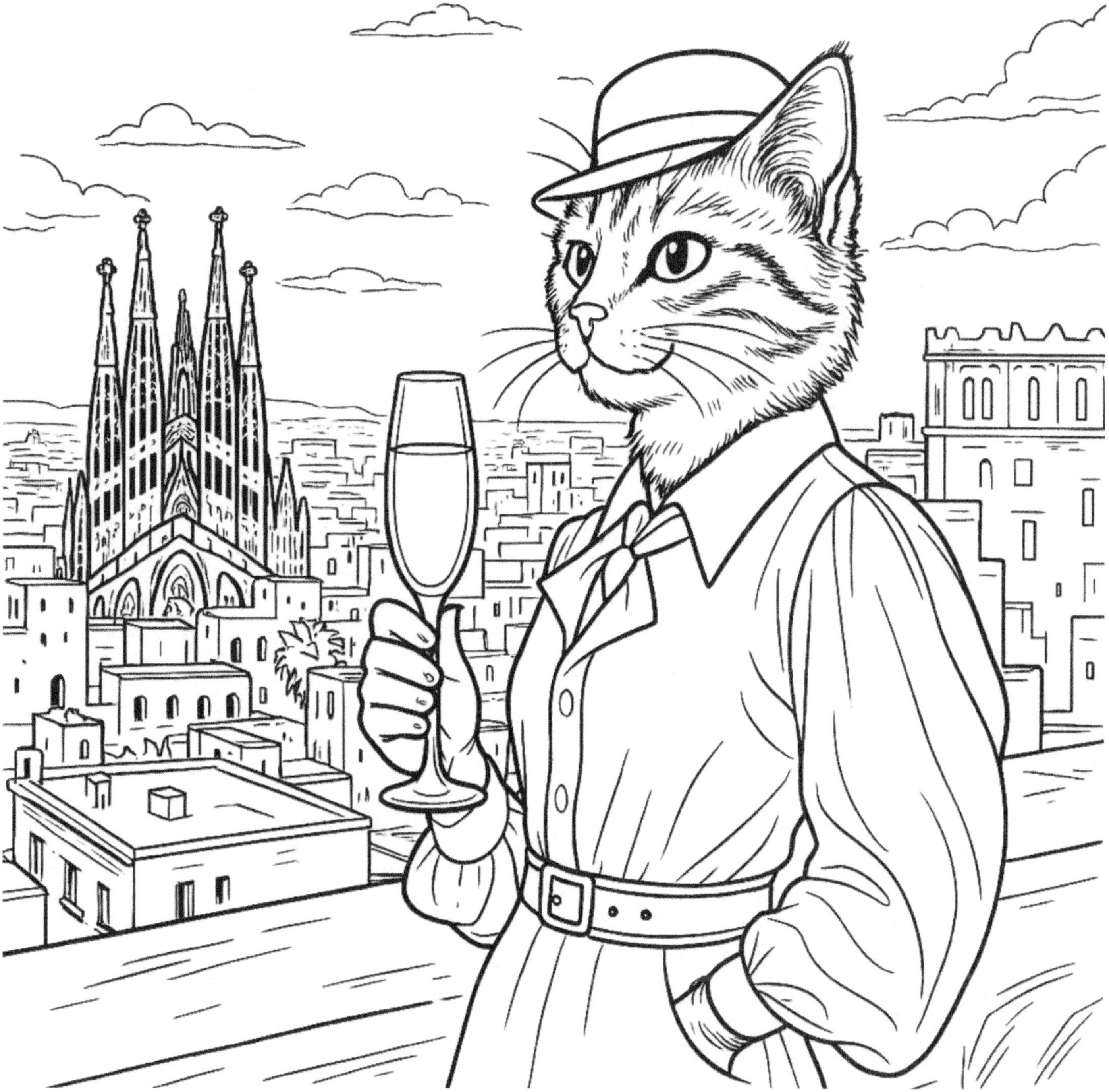

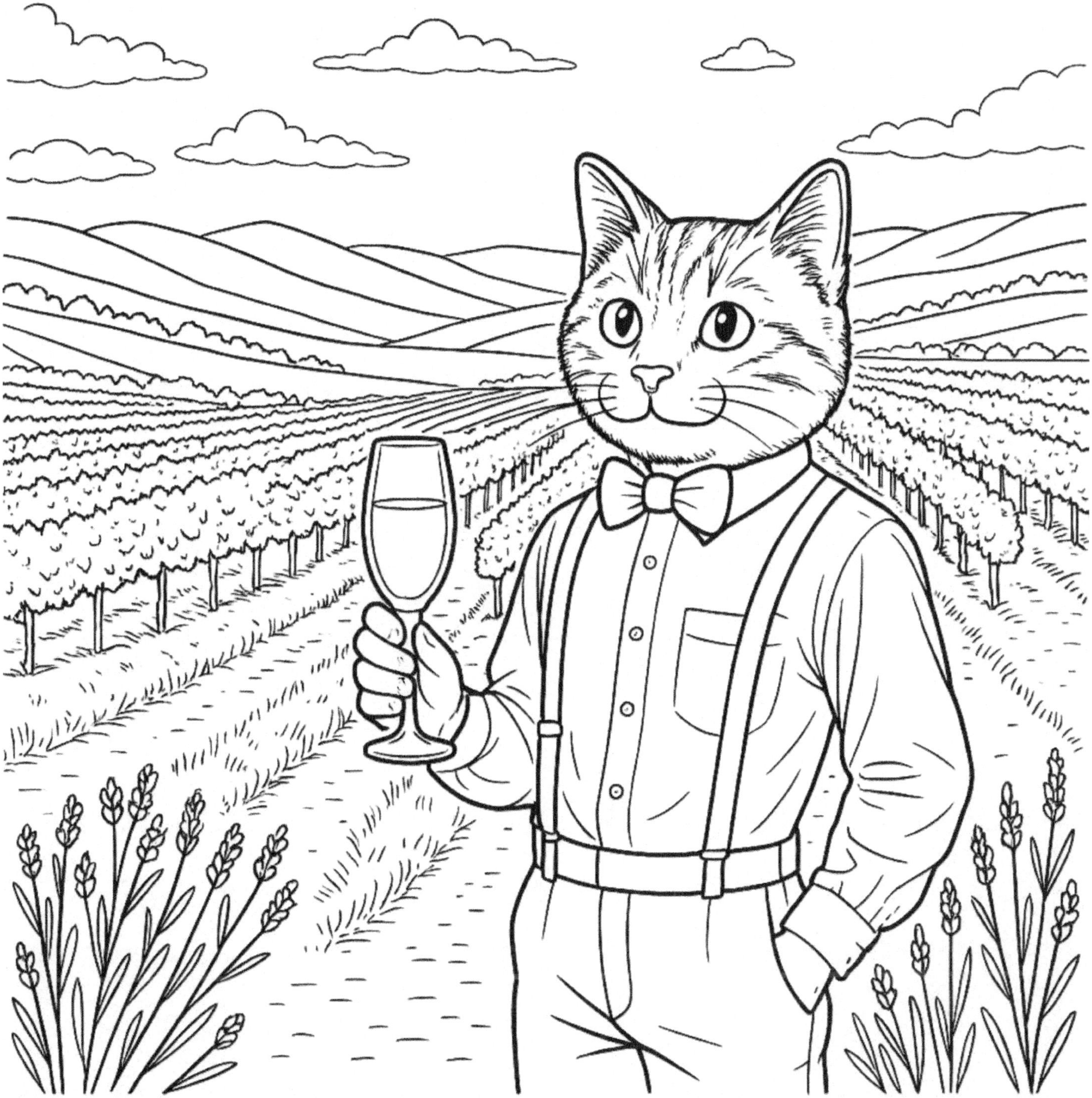

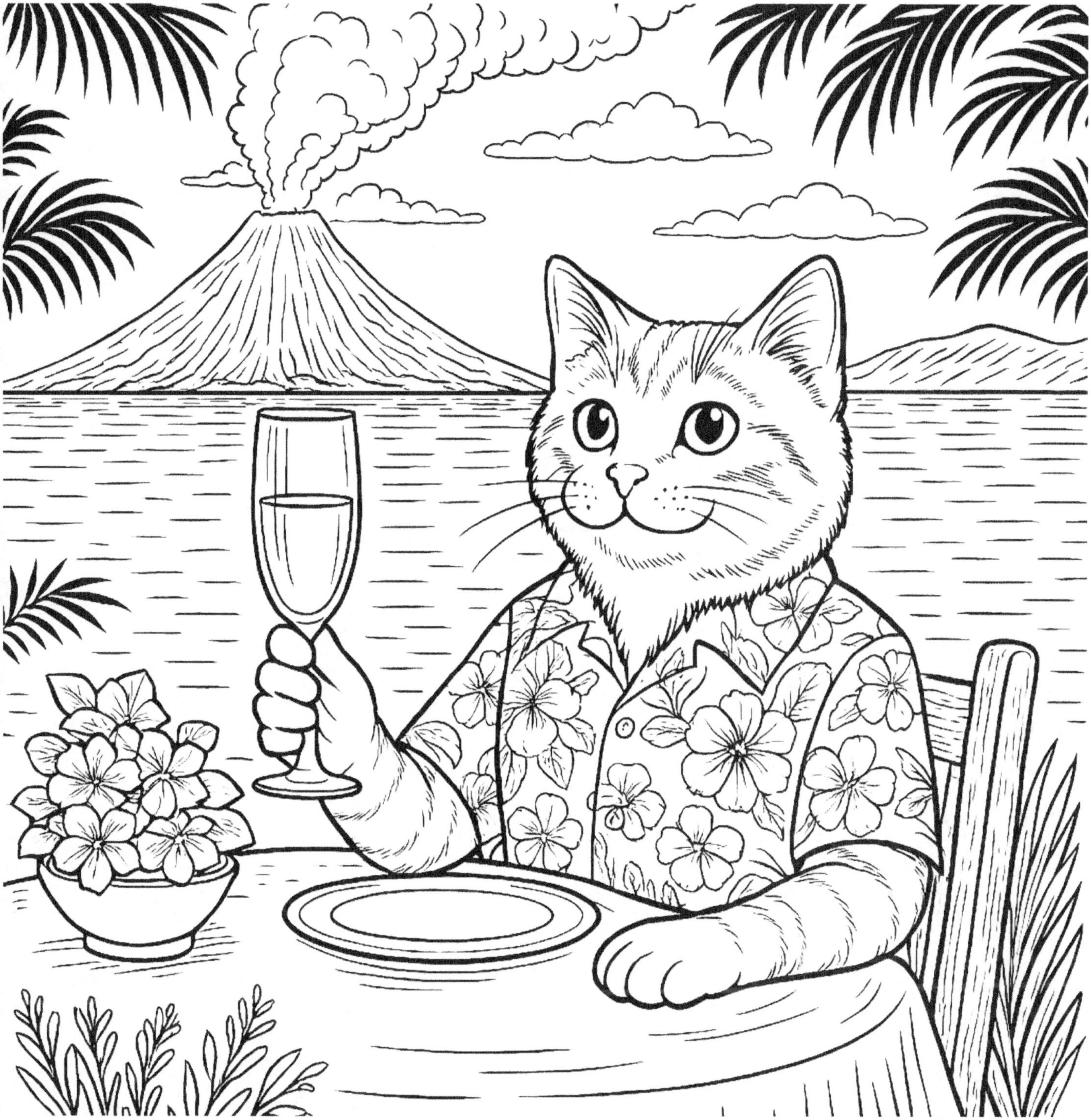

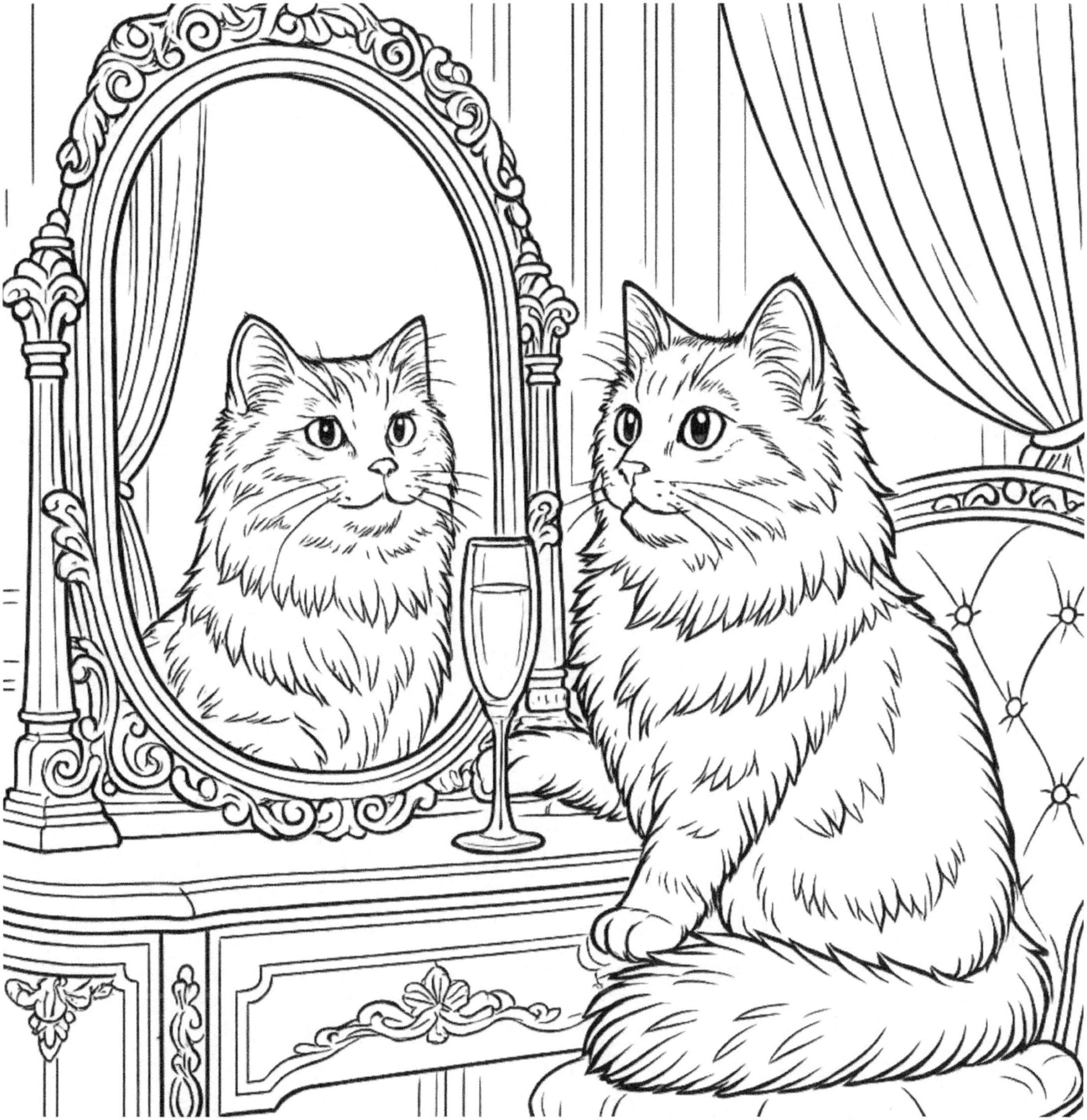

ACHR

@achrcreative

Printed in Dunstable, United Kingdom

65128098R00058